Baskets & Beyond

Baskets & Beyond

by Lucele Coutts

WATSON-GUPTILL PUBLICATIONS, NEW YORK

Edited by Sarah Bodine and Donna Wilkinson
Designed by Bob Fillie
Composed in 11/13 Century Medium by Copy Prep Company
Printed and bound by Interstate Book Manufacturers

Copyright © 1977 by Lucele Coutts

First published 1977 in the United States and Canada
by Watson-Guptill Publications,
a division of Billboard Publications, Inc.,
1515 Broadway, New York, N.Y. 10036

Library of Congress Cataloging in Publication Data
Coutts, Lucele.
    Baskets and beyond.
    Includes index.
    1. Basket making. I. Title.
TT879.B3C68   746.4'1   77–22379

ISBN 0–8230–0455–4

Manufactured in U.S.A.

First Printing, 1977

I dedicate this book
to the people who have helped me most—
Marion, Bill, and Stuart

ACKNOWLEDGMENTS

I wish to thank all the people named and unnamed who were helpful, tolerant, and lifted my spirits during the time I was researching and writing this book.

First, Doris Dietiker who started me in basketry, my students who were the guinea pigs for many of my theories, and some of my friends who proved helpful when instructions were too complex.

Marion Taylor Ward who had faith in my ability to write the book, Greta Jones and Carol Tickner who helped iron out a few wrinkles, Clinton MacKenzie who boosted my morale and gave me access to some student work, and the artists who have assisted me in completing the book by allowing me to use their work.

Most of all, I wish to thank my husband, Bill, who had ability to know what I needed in photography when I sometimes didn't, and my son, Stuart, who helped in proofreading, metric conversions, ideas, and all those unmentioned things which gave me the time to do what I did.

Most of the photography was shot by Bill Coutts; a few by Bob Burningham; and one by James Randkleve. Illustrations by Lucele Coutts.

Contents

Chinese Basket and Antique Chinese Tea Basket. The small piece shows the interesting base used for both baskets, in which the warps are extended out into a flat loop. The basket is plaited and twined. The large piece is an antique tea basket brought to this country by the China Clipper sailing ships. The tea basket is carried by the pickers who tie it over their shoulders with a cloth. It is plaited, with a three-strand twist weave used as a decorative element at the top, and the edge is wrapped.

Preface

When a friend suggested basketweaving as having possibilities for a contemporary sculptural medium, I became interested. After a few pieces, I found I was hooked.

Although my beginning pieces contained several complex ideas and sculptural problems that I ultimately solved, I felt I needed to go back to the simple beginnings to develop each facet of the craft step–by–step to build a good foundation. In so doing, I would be able to more thoroughly understand, and more properly use and teach it.

Incorporating only one color to a piece, I worked on many shaping and simple construction ideas before I felt satisfied enough to add each new dimension of color, texture, decorative materials, etc.

During this exploration period, I found a number of questions kept recurring, and I turned to the few available books for help. They were of substantial reputation in traditional basketweaving, but I was frustrated to find many of my questions went unanswered. For instance, not one book told how to finish a coiled basket. Searching the local museums helped little, and, in the end, I found most of the answers had to come from within myself.

As I developed new ideas and methods, I gave them to my students for testing. Adding, discarding, and refining as I moved along, I began to develop a system which seemed to work. I found, too, some people seemed to work well one way and some another, and so I have included duplicate systems which have worked successfully with both novice and experienced basketweaver.

While working on the book, more and more new ideas for weave variations and different uses for each technique kept flooding my mind. I have included all the new ideas I have tested and found workable.

With a happy heart I present this book to you with the hope you will find the excitement and fulfillment I have found in this reborn craft.

Chinese Sewing Basket. This type of basket was popular in the early 1900s. Some were decorated with money and beads; this basket has a scene painted on the lid. It is twined on the outside for strength and plaited on the inside for smoothness.

Introduction

Basketweaving, probably the oldest known textile craft, is coming of age. It is recognized as a link from the past that can be developed in a contemporary way.

Few materials and tools are needed. Anyone, anywhere, with access to a store or catalog can make a contemporary basket. Rope, yarn, a needle, a pair of scissors, and a happy heart are all that is needed. The beginning of a basket can be carried in a small bag, and as the work progresses, the materials may be carried in the basket itself.

Weaves may be few or many. Anything can be made with one or two weaves, but the more weaves and techniques learned, the more interesting and varied the results can be. A simple classic shape can become a textural experience with the addition of several weaves or a sprinkling of ornaments.

A Brief History. Basketweaving became highly developed in the primitive cultures, because the people were forced by necessity to construct houses, clothing, containers, and equipment from the materials found nearby. They had to make them with a limited number of tools, and oftentimes used parts of the body such as teeth, fingernails, hands, and feet.

Early in man's culture, basketweaving developed quickly to a fine degree of complex skills. Plaited baskets, simple and temporary, led the way to complex plaiting, as well as to twining and coiling. Coiling, the technique believed to be the highest degree of development in the craft, is not found in all cultures or tribes, but has been found throughout the world. Beautiful examples of coiled baskets that date back as far as 9000 B.C. have been found in North America and Africa.

The materials available were an important factor in the type of baskets made. In North America, two areas with widely varying climatic conditions had few types of basket fibers. Their differing solutions were determined by need, as well as the kinds of materials available.

The Aleutian Islands were abundant with good quality grasses. Since little else was available for their needs, the Aleuts made beautiful, delicately textured baskets. They were made to be used in varied ways.

On the mesas of the arid Southwest the few twigs and grasses were supplemented by an abundance of clay which would make fine containers. Here, baskets tended to be made for temporary use and for religious purposes.

In the area from San Francisco Bay north to Alaska many basket fibers were abundant. Grasses, reeds, roots, twigs, canes, split bark, leaves, and many other materials were available. Baskets were as abundant as the materials, and the need dictated the technique. Burden baskets were twined from large caned materials. Religious baskets or those which would be carefully handled were made slowly in the coiled technique of the finest materials and decorated with shells and feathers. Plaiting was rarely used. It was in this area that basketweaving reached its zenith in the Western Hemisphere.

Oneness with nature played an important role in the lives of the primitive basketweavers. They felt they were borrowing the materials needed, and returning them when finished with them. They gathered only what they needed; nothing was wasted. Present-day refuse: urine, animal droppings, ashes from the fire, were used as mordants to set the dye in the fibers or to dye the fibers for the new baskets. The only permanent tool, the sturdy awl, was made from leftover animal bone.

Basketmaking continued on through man's history, but, as he became industrialized, it was replaced by other crafts which could be mechanized, thus producing items more quickly. It was soon to become a lost art in most of the industrial world.

In the recent past in America when therapists began to recognize the need for people to work with their hands, basketweaving was introduced into programs for physical and mental rehabilitation. Playgrounds and schools included basketmaking as a "fun" project for children, but it was taken no further. The work produced this way was "pseudo-traditional," a copy of the past, with little or no thought of its meaning or the culture it represented. People felt the ultimate in basketweaving had been reached. There was a belief among authorities that any divergence from just "baskets" was wrong.

Basketweaving is a very personal craft. The piece of work grows out of and becomes an extension of the maker. To the traditional basketweaver it was and is a personal or religious experience understood only by the maker. Some weavers will not allow others to watch while they work. Many American Indian and African craftsmen are reluctant to teach outsiders or discuss their feelings about the work they do. Fortunately, a few of the native basketweavers are beginning to teach their craft. As they do, they are giving an understanding of their people and beliefs.

What Is the Future in Basketry? Today a new revival of basketweaving has come. It has been found again, but in a different way. It is a craft built from an essence of the past but growing out of today. Today's basketweavers are looking to the present for inspiration, to the life they live and understand. A new culture is developing. Hopefully, a growing together of the two cultures can be achieved as well, with a deeper understanding for all.

As mentioned before, there are three methods of basketweaving: plaited, twined, and coiled. All three will be covered in the book, but the emphasis will be on coiling techniques because they are best adapted to the contemporary materials available to most people.

In traditional basketweaving, all three of the methods made satisfactory baskets that were practical and structurally sound. In contemporary basketry, specific needs are not present, and the reeds, grasses, and roots have been replaced with contemporary materials. These materials have a control over the techniques used and over the final results.

Traditionally, plaiting is made by weaving with flat leaves or split woods. In this type of basketweaving, the material used gives the basket its form and structure. When switching to soft yarn fibers, woven fabric is the result. Therefore, choices of material must be made with this method in mind.

Twining, like plaiting, employs more of a weaving technique in the work. Traditionally, reeds, roots or grasses were woven or twined over a warp of canes or heavy grasses. Again, the material gave substance and body to the work. Lovely soft pieces can be achieved using this technique with yarns, but other warp materials will have to be used if sturdy baskets are to be the final outcome.

The ideal of all the basket techniques for contemporary materials is the coiled method. As coiling traditionally uses many kinds of plant fibers to produce a basket, it adapts easily to many kinds of ropes and yarns as well. Few variations are required in making the adjustment, and the structural strength is not impaired by the change to soft materials. With all of the types of commercial yarns and core materials available, the variations can be almost unlimited.

Since the native basketweavers tended to call all weaves basketweaves, there was a definite need for classification. Many of the weaves were classified by white Americans; therefore, most of the names assigned came from American Indian culture, although some came from Europe and Asia. Many of the names given were those of the tribes who worked most with a particular technique, although the weave may have been used elsewhere in the world. Some names came from the use of the weave. In this book, an attempt has been made to simplify classification and techniques in order to simplify instruction. The glossary of terms will give the common names and clarify their positions.

Basketweaving can be simple or complex. It can be practical or a flight into fancy. The projects included are for all degrees of difficulty. From simple and useful to fun and decorative, the directions are clear and concise enough to be understood by novice or experienced basketweaver.

With a little experience, the basketweaver will be able to move beyond baskets to make practical pieces that are not baskets, and useful items that are not containers. To those who want to be challenged further, the most exciting facet of all, sculptural basketry, is a complete free flight. The only remaining connection with the past is the technique which is making it possible, and the only remaining obstacle is how far one's imagination can reach. Now basketweaving has become an artform. It is contemporary, exciting, and mind–expanding.

Hanging Basket. 22½" x 13½" x 12" diameter (57.05cm x 34.29cm x 30.48cm). This is a coiled work basket to hold materials near the loom while weaving. The wrap is shades of brown cowhair–wool mix and variegated yellow to orange mohair over seven pieces of ¼" (.64cm) sized jute. The weaves are basic and pierced figure-eight.

Tools
and
Materials

1

Four things are important in the making of good baskets: the right attitude, the right materials, the right tools, and good craftsmanship.

There is a belief among traditional basketweavers that it is a privilege to make baskets. They feel they must be well and in a happy mood to produce the best work. This is very true. After the learning period is over, your hands seem to know what to do. As you work, your mind turns to other things. Good thoughts make your fingers fly and everything falls into place.

These first two chapters are probably the most important in the book. Your choices here will determine the end results of your work. All the tools and materials suggested for use in the book are good and useful, but they must be selected with the right techniques in mind to bring the expected results.

Chapter 1 discusses tools and equipment, and the myriad materials available today for making baskets. Chapter 2 covers items of interest for all types of basketweaving, instructions for making devices to aid your work, and general comments and advice to help you over the rough spots so you will bring a positive attitude to basketweaving.

You need few tools in basketweaving but each is important for its specific job. Equipment varies with the technique—plaiting, twining, or coiling—but some items can be used in all three. You probably have most of the necessary tools; and some of those suggested here are optional.

CUTTING TOOLS (PLAITING-TWINING-COILING)

If you are planning to focus your attention on one technique rather than on all three, choose the proper cutting tool for that technique as described below.

Blades. A cutter is a necessity in all three techniques. Use a sharp knife, single-edge razor blade, or X-Acto knife for leather, reed, and rope that are too heavy for scissors. Plant materials like reed, rope, and twine are very hard on blades. Do not use your kitchen knives unless you can sharpen them.

Scissors. Very sharp scissors made of a special alloy that does not have to be sharpened are available now in department, fabric, and hardware stores. They cut anything from fine fabrics to jute and other heavy rope products. Do not use scissors or similar cutters on reed, as they crush the material while cutting.

Wire Cutters. Another good tool for use on rope and twine is the versatile 6" to 7" (15.24cm to 17.78cm) wire cutter. Made of carborundum steel, this tool does not have to be sharpened and is very useful if you have good scissors that you do not want to use for cutting heavy materials. It is readily available in hardware stores.

PIERCING TOOLS (PLAITING-TWINING-COILING)

In contemporary basketry piercing tools are used to form a hole or to go through an existing opening. Find the proper tool for the technique you are employing.

Awls. In traditional basketry an awl was used to open a hole in the coiled baskets making way for the material to be pushed through. In contemporary basketry the awl is no longer used in coiling. It is used primarily in plaiting, but it can be used in twining to pierce a warp material to carry the weft material through. This is rarely done and can be handled in other ways.

To keep the awl point sharp in the tool box or work basket and protect yourself as well, keep a large cork on the tip. Awls can be purchased in hardware stores.

If you are a leather worker, you can use your leather punch instead of an awl in plaiting.

Needles. Needles are used for all three techniques. A needle is used to add edgings and decorative objects in plaiting. It is used to needle down or needle through in twining.

Primitive basketweavers used thorn needles in coiled basketry for fine materials which were difficult to push through the awl-punched holes. Some fine old baskets were wrapped 100 wraps to the inch (1" = 2.54cm).

In contemporary basketry the traditional awl has been replaced by tapestry needles for coiling. Since basketry is a weaving and not a sewing process, the use of needles is confusing to people. The needle allows two operations to be replaced by one. The needle forces an opening in the basket and carries the material through at the same time.

Needles are both blunt and sharp. The size of the basket and the type of material being used determines the length of the needle and the size of the eye. A rule of thumb is to choose a needle with an eye size large enough to carry the material and no more. The larger the eye the more difficult it is to pull through a tight place; and the more the basket is pulled apart to allow the needle to pass, the more it is weakened. If the material is flattened before threading on to the needle, heavier material can be threaded through than expected. Choose a needle long enough to handle easily when pulling through. Several blunt needlepoint and tapestry needles from 1½" to 4" (3.81cm to 10.16cm) in length are good to have on hand to use on different size baskets.

Sharpened tapestry needles with larger eyes are necessary for pierced

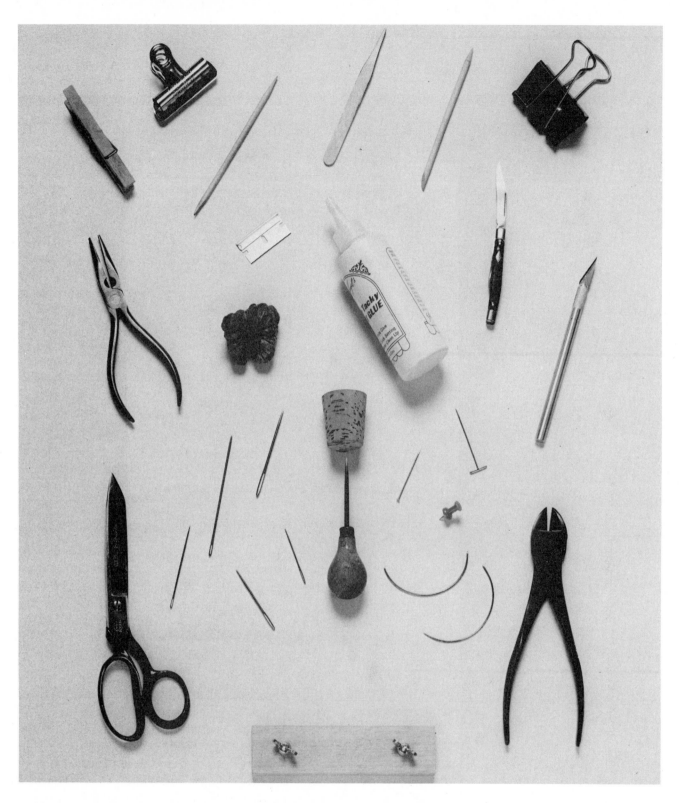

Tools and Equipment (left to right, top row). Pinch-type clothespin, bulldog clamp, orange stick from manicure set, tapered popsicle stick, orange stick, binder clamp. (Second row). Long-nose pliers, single-edge razor blade, beeswax, textile glue, sharp knife, X-Acto blade. (Third row). Scissors, sharp point tapestry needle, 4" (10.16cm) blunt tapestry needle, 2½" (6.35cm) blunt tapestry needle, 2½" (6.35cm) blunt needlepoint needle, 2" (5.08cm) blunt needlepoint needle, cork and awl, heavy shafted pin, push pin, T-pin, blunted curved needle, sharp curved needle, wire cutter. (Bottom center). Handmade wing-nut clamp.

weaves. An awl can be used to prepare the hole for a blunt needle to pass through, but this is a slow process.

Curved upholsterer's needles are very helpful in adding surface weaving, rya, or when working in tight corners. Curved needles are available in some needle kits in notions departments, but they tend to be rather small, are awkward to handle in tight places, and the eye is very narrow. The diameter of the curved needle remains the same within the area of the eye instead of swelling to allow more space for a larger eye as in the tapestry needle. A curved needle 2½" to 3" (6.35cm to 7.62cm) measured across from eye to tip is fine. Anything larger does not increase the eye size, and the extra length is awkward to control.

An upholsterer's shop will usually sell tools and supplies if they have extra on hand. They will sometimes order them for you when they place an order. Some upholsterer's supply houses will retail. Use your telephone book and be sure to call first.

Harness needles, bodkins, and balled-tip bent needles do not work in basketry. They are too wide, catch as they go through, and cut and tear.

All curved needles are sharp. To blunt a curved needle carefully cut off the tip into a wastebasket, shielding your eyes. A metal file stroked toward the tip will smooth off the rough edges.

MISCELLANEOUS TOOLS AND EQUIPMENT

There are various kinds of tools and equipment that do not fall into any specific category. These can be used in any one of the three techniques.

Pins (Plaiting-Twining). Heavy-shafted pins, T-pins, or wig pins about 1½" to 2½" (3.81cm to 6.35cm) long or pushpins with very long shafts are necessary to keep materials in place while plaiting or twining basket centers.

Pliers, optional (Twining-Coiling). A small pair of pliers is very helpful when pulling needles through tight places. The best type of plier is the long-nose variety because it slips into odd corners, but a small pair of any type will work. When pulling the needle through, keep it straight. Twisting or bending the needle when the eye is passing through a tight area can break it.

Prying Tools and Beaters (Plaiting-Twining). A prying tool is very helpful when reweaving in plaiting, whether inside the basket or on the decorative row on top of a previously woven row. An orange stick from a manicure set or a popsicle stick that has been narrowed and flattened make the best tools. They are easy to obtain, inexpensive, and most of all, they are gentle to the basket material.

An orange stick, a tapered popsicle stick, or a heavy tapestry needle make good beaters for twining.

Clamps (Plaiting-Twining-Coiling). Clamps hold plaiting on the frame, keep wefts and wraps from loosening while not working in twining and coiling, hold glued areas in plaiting until set, as well as many other little odd jobs that might come up.

The simplest and cheapest clamp that is universally available is the ordinary wooden pinch-type clothespin. Bulldog and binder clamps, available at stationery or office supply stores, cover more area when clamping plaited edges.

You can make a simple clamp for holding longer plaited edges. Use two thin, narrow boards, and two small bolts held by wing nuts. Drill two holes through both boards 1" (2.54cm) from each end, place the bolts in the holes, and fasten them with the wing nuts. Be sure to smooth the boards with sandpaper. The wing nuts can be fastened and unfastened with the fingers very quickly when in use.

Glue (Plaiting-Twining-Coiling). Use glue to splice leather and vinyl in plaiting, as well as to splice warps and cores in twining and coiling. In general, glue adds an extra hand to keep things under control until they can be completed in problem situations.

Textile glue is especially good to use because it remains flexible after drying, but any white glue can be used in moderation. Too much white glue will harden and become rigid. Do not use any kind of glue on the surface of the basket. It causes a color change and has a shiny look. When using glue on wefts and wraps, be sure the glued area is placed so it will not show on the surface.

Working Boards and Framing Materials (Plaiting-Twining). Celotex wallboard, acoustical tiles, heavy cardboard, corrugated cardboard boxes, Styrofoam, or a *hard* flat pillow made of sawdust or similar material make good working boards.

Fibers from wallboards rub off on clothing and materials. To keep them under control, cover the board with self-adhesive shelf or wall paper.

Chipboard, backs of writing tablets, corrugated boxes, old gift boxes, or popsicle sticks are good materials to use for plaiting frames.

MATERIALS

As the traditional basketweaver had to seek out, gather, properly prepare, and season the right materials to do a particular job, today's basketweaver must choose the proper materials that are available from the merchant's overflowing shelves to make the pursuit of basketweaving a joy. Wherever you go, whatever you are doing, keep an eye out for possible materials. You will find them in the most unlikely places. When you have to search for materials, you will become more inventive, and you will find things you might otherwise overlook. It is quite exciting to find surprises around every corner.

Some materials are inexpensive and some expensive. Do not ignore the expensive materials. Use them in small amounts to make an ordinary basketform extraordinary.

Since specialty shops are located in some large cities, the materials available through them are described on p. 21. Without personally visiting each store across the country, it is difficult to give an honest assessment of the inventories available, and even familiar shops change their inventories frequently. The telephone book is a great help in finding specialty shops. Your local high school or adult school craft teachers can be a help in locating specialty shops in your area, especially if you live in a small town.

A short list of stores and companies that handle specialty materials is

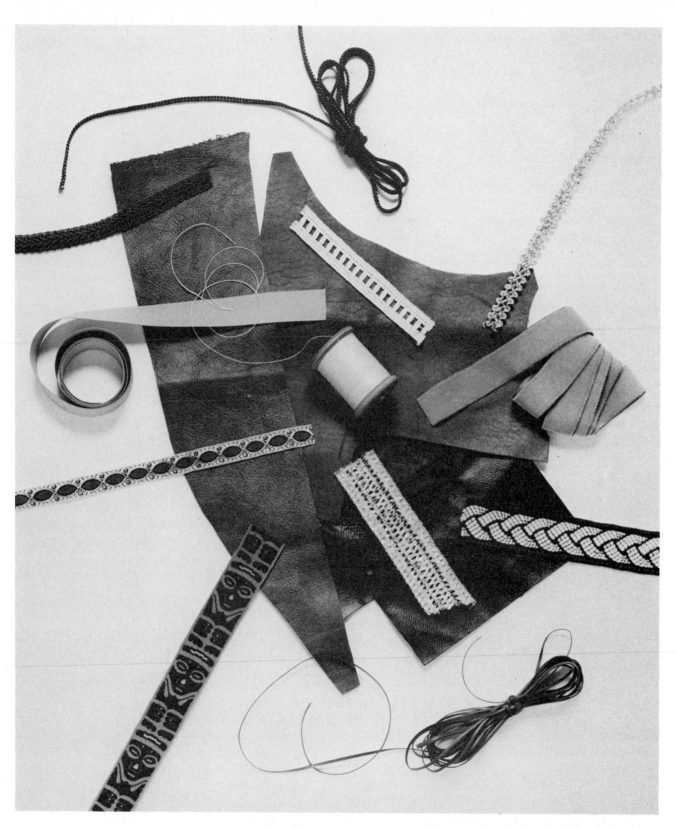

Materials for Plaiting. The top butterfly is synthetic macrame braid. The background materials are (clockwise from left), vinyl upholstery fabric, wallet weight cowhide, wallet weight goat. The braids and ribbons are (clockwise from top left), synthetic coiled braid, lace gimp braid, gold metallic braid, velvet ribbon, woven braid, plastic woven braid, woven braid, synthetic and metallic woven braid, grosgrain ribbon. In the center is a spool of linen thread, and the bottom butterfly is leather lacing.

given in the back of this book. These stores will mail order; some have catalogs and some do not.

More good places to investigate are: grocery, department, hardware, marine hardware, boat supply, fabric, plastic, and variety stores; weaving, needlework, needlepoint, macrame, knitting, yarn, art supply, thrift, upholstery repair, antique repair, hobby, leather, and welding shops; farm, building, rope, upholstery, and medical supply houses; lumberyards, garage, and rummage sales.

Each of the basketweaving techniques described in this book is covered in relation to contemporary materials. There has been no attempt to develop traditional concepts or methods unless they have a direct relationship to contemporary basketweaving. In order to break away from traditional thinking in basketry, it is necessary to break away from traditional materials. We must look for new ways to use this marvelous ancient craft in today's world with today's ideas. After this is learned, we may turn to the more traditional materials to use them in a contemporary way.

The size, weight, flexibility, and content of the materials can direct, help, or hinder the basketweaver. Materials are divided into three general categories: materials for plaiting, materials for warps and cores, and materials for wefts and wraps.

MATERIALS FOR PLAITING

Plaiting, the simplest and probably earliest known technique, is a woven method using torn and cut ribbonlike leaf strips. Its construction requires attractive material because every strip is visible. Leaf strips are attractive and practical and hold onto each other during the weaving process. After the basket is finished, an overnight soaking releases the cellulose material which hardens and helps to fasten the strips together even tighter. Traditionally plaiting material is abundant and is structurally strong enough to make a useful basket.

Today's plaiting materials are not as abundant, are not as easily controlled, and most are fairly expensive, but there are some fine materials which work well. Although a personal preference leaves most of plaiting within the traditional area, there are some interesting things that can be done. Your basketforms will be rich and extraordinary.

Possible materials for plaiting are: leather, vinyls, ribbons, braids, metallic bands and braids, and strips of metal, precious and nonprecious. Not all of these materials are strong, but they can be used in various ways successfully.

Leather. Leather is attractive, comes in many colors, is easily available, can be cut without difficulty, and handles nicely. It comes in many weights, and it can be marked and cut into any desired width and length. It has enough body to make a structurally sound piece. The results are rich and beautiful.

Leather is cheapest by the hide or hide piece. It can be purchased in strips, although the sizes are limited, the type of leather is limited, and it is expensive. Hides can be cut with sharp scissors or a sharp single-edge razor blade according to the weight of the leather. Leather has rough and smooth surfaces.

It is available through leather shops, supply houses, and hobby shops. These stores are in larger cities primarily, but there is a chain of leather shops throughout the country. They are in smaller towns and they sell leather supplies by mail (see the Suppliers List). Leather can be found at thrift shops, garage sales, and rummage sales.

Vinyls. Vinyl plastics come in many forms. The most common and most attractive is the vinyl upholstery fabric that simulates leather. It is strong, sturdy, and easily cut. It is available in upholstery and fabric shops, department stores, and through catalogs.

Decorative Materials. Decorative braids are flexible, fairly strong, and heavy, but they are expensive. Ribbons, laces, and other similar materials are soft and flexible. These materials do not work well by themselves because the result is soft like cloth, but they can be introduced into leather and vinyl baskets and handbags as a decorative material without weakening the structure. Some of these specialty materials can be used in coiling for plaited areas or imbrications. The notions department of fabric and department stores carry many decorative materials for plaiting. Heavy braided macrame cords also make beautiful decorative accents in coiled baskets.

Metal Strips. If you like working in metals, strips of metal can create beautiful basketforms. This material is expensive, but the baskets made from it can be useful in a number of ways: interior and exterior planters (hanging and standing), kitchen baskets, and wastebaskets. Charming

Using Metal in Basketweaving. This plaited basket 1½" x 4" x 4" diameter (3.81cm x 10.16cm x 10.16cm) is a satisfactory experiment to show what can be done with soft flexible ¼" (.64cm) metal strips using only basketweaving tools. The little coiled starts are made with 18 gauge copper wire for the core and 24 gauge copper wire for the wrap. Metal tools produce more finished looking pieces.

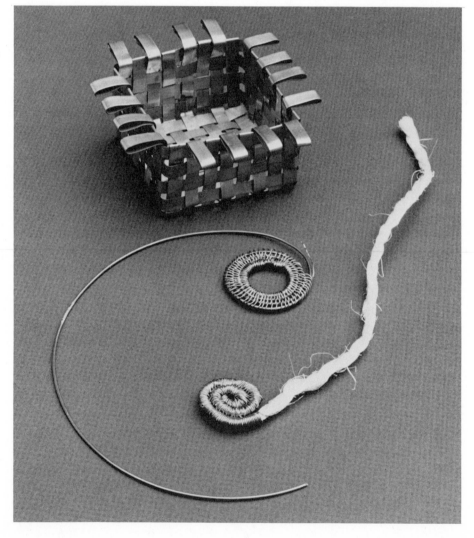

little boxes and containers for practical or ornamental use make an interesting change of pace.

Jewelers can work with precious metals using basketry techniques with really exciting results. This area will be only lightly touched in this book because it is an entirely different field using different tools, equipment, and materials.

Lacing Materials. Leather and plastic lacing, round braids, and heavy linen cords are the best materials for lacing and edging. Leather lacing is best to use with leather, but other materials are attractive as well, if the colors and materials work together.

Linen cords, crochet thread, cotton rug warps, and other heavy materials that will not break easily when tightened will work, but linen will withstand time best. Waxing these materials before using eliminates tangling and breaking.

Leather and plastic lacing can be found at leather stores and some hobby shops. Braids, threads, and cords can be found at macrame stores, sewing notion counters, and some catalog houses. Beeswax is available at sewing notions counters and upholstery supply or repair shops.

If you have trouble finding round braids, you can spool knit or spool braid your own with crochet thread of any color.

MATERIALS FOR WARPS AND CORES

There are many cylindrical, ropelike materials available for warps in twining and for cores in coiling. Since the base materials are usually covered completely with both techniques, they do not have to be attractive.

Twining requires a beating process to force the woven wefts together on the warps. Therefore the material used for the warp must be almost fiber free. The cores in coiling can be any type of ropelike material that is fibrous, flexible, and not necessarily attractive. Plied material allows for strand separation when working with freeform sculpture in coiling and twining.

Materials available are: jute, manila and sisal hemp, plastic and braided clothesline, polyvinyl tubing, fiber rush, sea grass, reed, plastic-covered wire, cotton seine cord, synthetic ropes, brazier rods, and heavy gauge flexible wire.

Jute (Coiling). Jute is a medium weight, inexpensive plied rope. It has a smooth surface. It is flexible, fibrous, and comes in many sizes. Its quality ranges from a rough and uneven material filled with plant impurities to a bleached and tightly twisted high-quality material. Jute ropes can be grouped together to make a core of a larger size. Although smooth, most of it is too fibrous for twining; high-quality jute can be used with care. However, it is excellent for cores in coiling. A slight stroking of the jute away from the wrapping will keep the fibers under control. It is available in macrame supply shops, art stores, marine hardware and rope supply stores, hardware stores, some department stores, and some weaving shops.

Sisal and Manila Hemp (Open-Coiled Weaving, Twining, and Coiling). These materials come from the same plant family, although the Mexican sisal is lighter in color than the Asian manila or hemp, as it is sometimes called. They are usually plied and have a rough rippled surface. Less fibrous than jute, the stiff fibers are more easily controlled in weaving. These materials are rigid and strong, and attractive.

Materials for Warps and Cores.

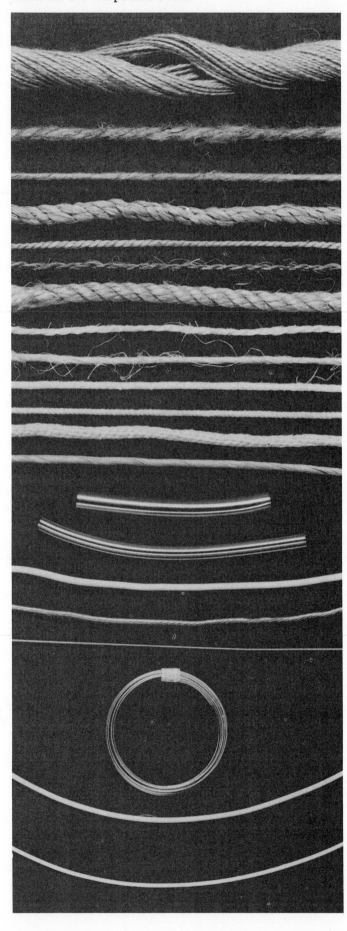

high quality 1" (2.54cm) jute

poor quality ⅜" (.95cm) jute

high quality ¼" (.64cm) jute

3-ply munj (Pakistan)

sea grass
côir (Srilanka)

3-ply manila

2-ply sisal

single ply sisal

braided clothesline

seine cord

braided clothesline

fiber rush

two thicknesses
of polyvinyl tubing

plastic clothesline

plastic covered wire

brass brazier (welder's) rod

16 gauge brass wire

two thicknesses of reed

Sisal is available in single ply (used for tying newspaper bundles, etc.) and in loose bulk form. The loose sisal can be hand spun to any size. These ropes are heavier in weight and cleaner than jute and thereby more expensive.

In coiling, the stiffness of these materials can make starting a basket difficult. If it is too hard to bend the material around, use a softer product, like jute, as the core until the material can be bent easily. Splice the stiffer material on to the softer material as soon as possible (see Tapering and Splicing in Chapter 2). This technique was used by traditional basketweavers.

On the finishing of a basket the stiff fibers may give you some difficulty. Taper the material very gradually, and lay some glue along the tapered edge. Let it dry. This will keep the stiff fibers under better control while wrapping over them.

Clothesline Ropes (Twining and Coiling). Clothesline is available in many forms and colors. Plastic lines come with hollow centers, fiber-filled centers, and wire-reinforced fiber-filled centers. Cotton braided ropes come in several forms as well. Some are loose fiber-filled and others have plyed material in the center. Some are covered with a synthetic braiding. Large smooth plastic-covered ropes can make beautiful core materials.

Both plastic and cotton clotheslines are clean, smooth, light in weight, flexible, and in the medium price range. The plastic line splices and tapers easily, while the braided material needs a little more care (see Tapering and Splicing in Chapter 2).

These materials are available in hardware, grocery, department, drug, and variety stores.

Polyvinyl Tubing (Open-Coiled Weaving, Coiling, and Twining). This material is attractive, clean, clear, hollow, and flexible. Sometimes it has a slight color cast toward yellow or blue-violet. It comes in many sizes and weights, and the walls of the tube can be thick or thin. The heavier the weight, however, the more expensive it is and the less readily available. Polyvinyl tubing can be found in plastic supply stores and medical supply houses.

It can be used in either technique, but it is especially good for open-coiled weaving. Strands of yarn can be threaded through the tubing for extra effect.

Fiber Rush (Twining and Coiling). Fiber rush, also known as paper rush, is used primarily for woven rush seats. It is a heavy, treated paper material, twisted into a single ply. Light in weight, it is rigid, strong, and medium priced. It can be found in basket supply, upholstery supply, craft, and weaving supply, or antique repair shops.

Plastic-Covered Wire (Coiling). Plastic-covered wire is a material found in hardware stores, nurseries, building supply, and department stores. It is a strong material used to tie up objects which need to be protected at the same time, such as support lines for young trees. It must be cut with wire cutters, and pliers are needed for tight bends. This material is rigid, comes in colors, usually green, is heavy in weight, and expensive. It is recommended only for special heavyweight coiled pieces. It has to be taped to be spliced, and finishing off takes extra care. A good material to use in stress areas for extra strength, plastic-covered wire works well for very large pieces that have open spacing in the body of the basket (slits, gaps, etc.).

Cotton Seine Cord (Twining and Coiling). Seine cord comes in many sizes, is lightweight, clean, inexpensive, flexible, and plyed. It is available in hardware, drug, and variety stores, and marine hardware and macrame shops.

Upholsterer's Roving (Coiling). Roving is deceptive. Although it is large in size, it packs down when wrapped. In the medium to high price range, roving is lightweight and works well when combined with stiffer material for a larger core in coiling. It is available in upholstery supply and repair stores.

Synthetic Rope (Coiling and Twining). Synthetic rope is strong, easily unraveled, medium priced, and medium to heavy in weight. It is best used in coiling because it can be difficult to finish off the ends in twining, although the ends can be left uncovered as part of the basket design (see Chapter 7). It is available at boat supply, marine hardware, and hardware stores.

Reed, Rattan (Coiling and Twining). Reed, also known as cane, comes in many sizes, and is strong, rigid, attractive, durable, and lightweight. It splices easily, but must be soaked to bend well. Since it is difficult to bend for basket centers, you must use a softer fiber to start a coiled basket. In the medium price range, reed is available in basketry supply, antique, and upholstery repair stores.

Sea Grass (Open-Coiled Weaves, Coiling, and Twining). Sea grass is attractive, fragrant, and lightweight. It is a plied material, comes in limited sizes, is expensive, and has limited availability. It is available at basketry supply stores, upholsterer's, and antique repair shops.

Munj (Coiling and Twining). Munj is a special plied material made from palm leaves. It comes in different sizes, is a light creamy color, and is very attractive. It is available through specialty shops.

Heavy-Gauge Flexible Wire (Coiling and Twining). Aluminum, copper, brass, and steel wire require wire cutters for cutting. This wire is available at hardware stores, welding shops, building suppliers, and some lumberyards. It should be used with a finer-gauge wire as the wrap. Pliers are needed for tight bends.

MATERIALS FOR WEFTS AND WRAPS

Materials for the wefts in twining and the wraps in coiling must be flexible enough to twist and wrap tightly. There are many types of yarn materials available which are strong, attractive, come in many colors, and are good for both techniques.

These materials can be found in department stores, needlework, weaving, knitting, yarn, and thrift shops, garage and rummage sales, macrame shops, and basketry supply stores.

Animal Fibers (Twining and Coiling). There are many animal fibers available for use in baskets. The largest group of animal fibers, wool, comes in many weights, types, and colors, As yarns are spun with specific uses in mind, the materials should be chosen to fit a specific technique.

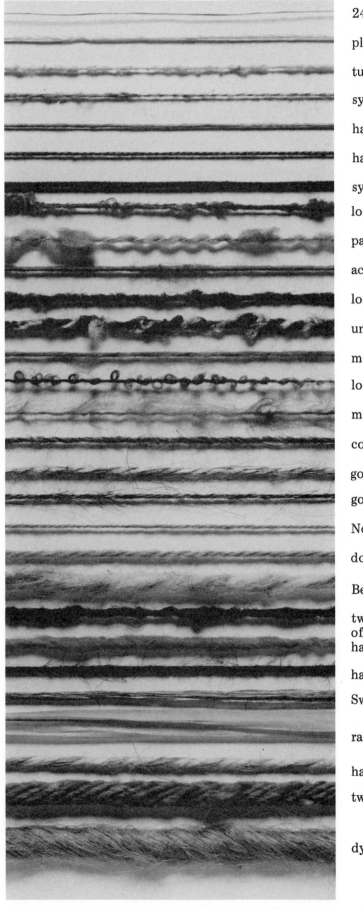

24-gauge copper wire

plyed plastic twine

tussah (wild) silk

synthetic-linen mix

hard twist linen

hard twist weaving rayon

synthetic imitation chenille

loose spun synthetic

partially looped synthetic

acrylic

loose spun synthetic

uneven spun synthetic

mohair-wool mix

looped mohair

mohair

cow hair–wool mix

goat hair–synthetic mix

goat hair

Norwegian rug wool

domestic rug wool

Berber wool

two thicknesses
of Pakistani
handspun wool

hard twist dyed jute

Swiss straw

raffia

hard twist linen (heavyweight)

tweed wool ¼" (.64cm)

dyed craft jute ¼" (.64cm)

Elastic yarns work well in twining, but nonelastic yarns should be used in coiling, if possible. The warp in twining must be quite strong in order to carry the weight of the piece, but any type yarn can be used in the weft. In coiling, however, the wrap is the glue that fastens the basket together, and the weight of the basket and its contents are carried by the fastening wraps; therefore these must be the strong elements.

If elastic yarns are used in coiling, you can strengthen the basket in several ways: wrap the material very tightly; double or triple the strands of material; use a strand of nonelastic yarn with a strand of elastic yarn. There are many nonelastic yarns available so the problem is not great.

While knitting yarns are elastic, the best overall nonelastic yarn for strength is rug wool. Rug wools come in many weights and sizes, both domestic and imported. Also there are handspuns, Mexican yarns, and weaving wools of many weights.

Silk, camelhair, mohair, angora, cowhair, and goathair are some other animal fibers. Some of these fibers come in pure form, others will be combined with other fibers to strengthen them, due to the fact that some fibers cannot be spun alone because they are too short, too coarse, or too smooth to spin well. These fibers are combined with wools, synthetics, and linens. Special animal fibers come in many weights and sizes from very fine to heavy handspuns. They are available in bulk as well if you want to spin your own fiber.

Plant Fibers (Twining and Coiling). The plant fibers are cotton, linen, ramie, jute, raffia, coir, and munj. Cotton comes in many forms: rug warps, rug yarn, handspuns, and in bulk for spinning. Cotton is used to blend with other fibers, such as cottolin, a mixture of cotton and linen. Cotton shreds off when used in coiling unless the material is a hard twist.

Linen comes in different weights, sizes, and textures. There are some fine cords and hard twist linen thread available in macrame shops. They make beautiful, natural baskets.

Ramie is a material with the strength of linen and the sheen of cotton. It is difficult to process and thus rare. It can be found in some mixes, and is available occasionally in bulk. Weaving and yarns shops are the best source.

Raffia is a specialty leaf material. Available in colors including its original creamy color, it will give a natural look to your work. It is usually recommended that the fingers be dampened when using raffia. Personal experience has found this unnecessary, although the raffia must be constantly twisted as you work or it has a tendency to split and break. The twisting gives a smoother look as well. Strong, smooth, slightly shiny, raffia has a waxy feel. It is available in basketry or macrame stores, hobby shops, and specialty craft shops.

Coir is an inexpensive plyed cord made of coconut fiber. Coarse like twine, it has a very natural look and is available in some basketry, macrame, and weaving shops.

Munj (palm leaves made into twine) can be used as a weft or wrap in the lightweight size.

Synthetics (Coiling and Twining). Synthetic yarns are extremely varied. Industry has been able to create chemically almost every natural fiber and the end results are pleasing and useful. From exciting specialty yarns to sturdy rug yarns, the choice is great. The synthetic yarns are both elastic and nonelastic.

Specialty Yarns (Twining and Coiling). There are some interesting specialty yarns that can be used in baskets. Mohair, bouclé, looped yarns, thick and thin, bumpy and nubby yarns, and unusual mixtures of all types can be found in yarn stores. These yarns are more fragile than the smooth yarns and must be handled in special ways. Twining is less abusive to delicate yarns than coiling. With care, some of these yarns can be used in coiling with beautiful results, but not in pierced weaves. The constant pulling and dragging tears the yarns apart and they become ragged. Directions for handling delicate yarns are found in Chapter 2.

Swiss Straw (Coiling and Twining). Swiss straw is a synthetic material which can be used in the same way as raffia. It is very shiny, comes in bright colors, and is inexpensive. It is available in needlework, fabric, yarn, and specialty craft stores. Like raffia, it will split and needs to be twisted as you work.

Fur (Coiling and Twining). Fur can be obtained from pelts, such as rabbit pelts which can be found in some novelty stores. Look for old fur coats at rummage sales, garage sales, and thrift shops. Some thrift shops have pieces of fur that cannot be used by furriers. Ask friends for castoffs.

If you cannot find real fur or do not want to use it, there are many kinds of artificial furs that are interesting. These are available in upholstery shops, department stores, and fabric stores.

Small Gauge Flexible Wire (Coiling and Twining). Small gauge wire in copper, brass, aluminum and steel can be found in hardware stores. It can be cut with wire cutters and worked by hand. However, it must be handled carefully to keep it from twisting or knotting. If bent in the same place too many times it will break.

Peacock Feather Basket. 17" x 11" (43.18cm x 27.94cm). This attractive multiarrangement basket was made by Nancy Kull of Long Beach, California. Woven in basic figure-eight, it is braided clothesline wrapped in green acrylic rug yarn. After separating the barbs of the peacock feathers, she wrapped them with monofilament fishing line and fabricated them onto the basket.

Information and Advice

2

The following list will provide you with a few simple rules for basket-weaving.

1. *Start small.* Your work will grow in strength and control. Watch the improvement piece by piece. Save your ambitious pieces until your muscles become stronger and your techniques are at your fingertips.

2. *Learn a technique well and develop it further.* Try to work at length in different weaves. This will educate your fingers to do the job. Once the technique is learned, your hands will know what to do.

3. *Be flexible in your ideas.*

4. *Turn out a product that is as well-crafted as your present ability allows.* As your ability grows your craftsmanship should grow as well.

5. *Choose the proper materials for the techniques and the weaves.*

6. *Enjoy your work as it progresses.*

HANDEDNESS IN BASKETRY

Plaiting and twining work easily whether you use the dominant hand or not, but coiling can become a problem if you try to work with the other hand. Left-handed people have a tendency to try to work in crafts with the right hand because the directions are always for the right hand. In coiling, this can prove difficult because a certain strength is needed that only the dominant hand can provide.

Although the illustrations in this book are made for right-handed people, the written directions deal with the working hand and the holding hand. This eliminates one problem. Of course, all of these problems are solved if you have the ability to reverse the illustration mentally. If you are not able to do this, hold the page up to a strong light and look through the back of the page. The illustration will be reversed.

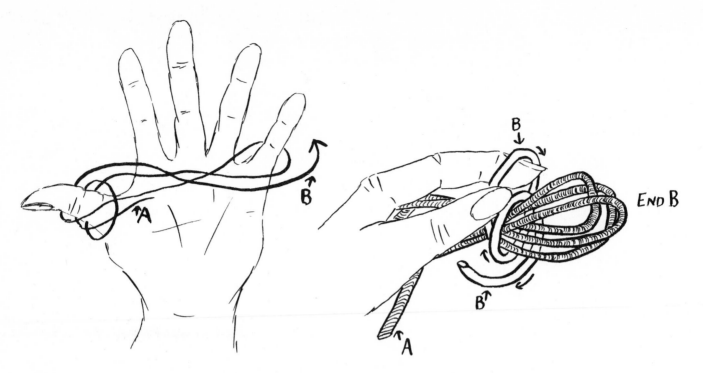

Making a Butterfly, Step 1. Make figure-eights around the little finger and thumb until about 12" (30.48cm) remains on B end.

Step 2. Wrap strand B over the index finger and around butterfly. Continue wrapping strand B around the butterfly under index finger until 6" (15.24cm) remains.

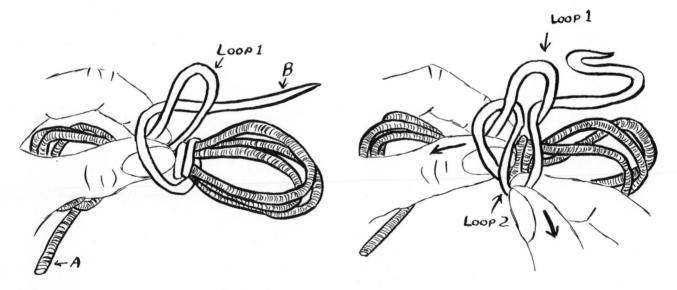

Step 3. Slip index finger out of the loop, but do not release the strand from fingertips. Carry strand B around loop to the back.

Step 4. From the front pull strand B through loop 1 which will form loop 2.

PREPARING WEFTS AND WRAPS

To begin a plaited or twined basket, all the warps are cut and ready before the center of the basket is woven. In coiled basketry, the ball or reel of core is ready for use. Why not ready the wefts and wraps in the same way? It saves time and effort later, and the work goes ahead more smoothly without interruptions.

Preparing Wefts for Plaiting and Twining. The wefts can be cut and ready to weave into a plaited basket when needed because the total amount to be used is known ahead of time, unless the shape is unusual or asymmetrical.

To plan the amount of material needed in twining is not as easy, but if you make several butterflies (see below) ahead of time, they will then be ready for use when needed.

BUTTERFLIES

Butterflies are used for three things in basketweaving. In twining, they are used as weavers. In coiling, particularly in Method 2 of the ripple weave, one piece of core and one piece of wrap must be held out of the way while working with the other two pieces in each row. The butterflies keep the extra material out of the way. Also in coiling, the strands of a multi-strand core must be kept straight to keep a smooth surface on the row. If each strand is made into a butterfly, the strands are less apt to twist and tangle. When they do tangle they can be straightened out quickly.

The following method of making a butterfly was learned from Helga Miles, a master weaver from Germany. It is a different and practical way to produce a secure butterfly that will stay fastened in position by itself without other devices. When undone, it leaves no knot. This butterfly requires a little patience to learn, but once learned you will see it is as easy as tying your shoe when one shoestring is too short to make a complete bow.

Making a Butterfly. You will be working with two types of material: attached (to the basket in progress) and unattached. If you are working with attached material, start the directions at the end closest to the basket.

Step 1. Wrap end A of the material around the thumb two or three times (this end will be the working end of the butterfly). Now make figure eights around the little finger and the thumb (this end will be used to fasten the butterfly together and will be called B).

If the material is about the weight of four-ply knitting yarns, stop making the figure eights when about 12" (30cm) extends out from the B end (more length is needed for a heavier material, less for lighter material).

Step 2. Grasp the butterfly by the center crossing from the top with the working hand, and carefully remove the butterfly from the holding hand without letting it slip apart. Let the end A strand fall free. Firmly grasp the butterfly with the holding hand between the thumb and the third finger leaving the index finger free. Extend the index finger over the crossing, toward the B end of the butterfly.

Pick up the end B strand and place tightly between the index finger and the tip of the thumb making sure the strand is slightly separated from the body of the butterfly. Do not release this strand during the whole operation. Loop the end B strand over the index finger and on around the butterfly. Now wrap *under* the index finger and around the butterfly until there is about 4" to 10" (10 to 25cm) left (according to the weight of the material).

Step 3. Slip the index finger out of loop 1 without releasing the strand from the fingertips. Take the end B strand around the holding hand side behind loop 1 and drop.

Step 4. Pull the end B strand through loop 1 from the front to form loop 2. Pull loop 2 and loop 1 to tighten. To use, pull the material from end A.

If the butterfly is thick, it will eventually loosen as the material is pulled out of it. Undo the bow when this happens, tighten the wrapping, and retie the bow as before.

PREPARING WRAPS FOR COILING

In coiling, lengths must be cut to use in wrapping the core. Although you will not know exactly how much material you will need for the entire basket, you can cut enough lengths to make up a ball or two that will keep you supplied for some time.

Planning the Wrap Length. The length of the material to be used in coiling is determined by a number of things: your experience as a basketweaver, the size of the core, and the stability of the material.

The usual length of the coiling wrap is three to four lengths. A length is the distance you can pull the material out to the side or an arm length. This length is about a yard (meter). Since the wrap in coiling has a tendency to tangle, it is recommended that inexperienced basketweavers use shorter lengths until they learn how to handle this problem. One arm length is fine to start.

If the core is larger than ½" (12.7mm), more length should be measured off. Large cores eat up the wrap quickly. A small basket with core under ½" (12.7mm) might take ¾" (19.05mm) of the material for each wrap, but a large piece of core 1" (2.54cm) or more in diameter will use 2½" (6.35cm) or more per wrap. Measure off four to six arm lengths for use with large cores—more than six arm lengths is awkward to use.

How to Control the Wrap Tangling. The wrapping motion in coiling twists the material. This twisting either causes the material to unply or overply according to the direction of the yarn twist in the original spinning. Left- and right-handed people twist in opposite directions as they work. Watch the material as you work. If the material untwists and the plys begin to loosen, twist it back. If the material kinks up, you have overtwisted it, and must allow it to untwist. Twirling the needle between the fingers or allowing the material to hang loose, weighted with the needle, will return it to its proper position again.

The material always has a tendency to catch a little as it is being pulled through. Be careful that the yarn does not unply too far, as the extra yank needed to pull it through may break it.

PREVENTING FRAYED ENDS AND DAMAGE

Besides the problem of yarns unplying too far and thereby breaking, there are other characteristics of basketweaving materials which may cause them to break or fray.

Frayed Rope Ends. Some rope materials untwist easily. Synthetic ropes, cotton seine cord, and similar materials can be a problem. In thin materials it is possible to tie a knot in the end, but thicker materials must be wrapped with tape to keep the ends intact. When tapering the ends, glue will keep the end fibers in place and out of the way of the wrapping. Touching the ends of synthetic materials with a match or gas flame will melt the ends together. However, be careful because too much heat for too long a time will darken or burn the plastic material.

Protecting Delicate Materials from Damage. It is easy to damage loose and uneven yarns while coiling. Handspuns, yarns with uneven spinning, bouclés, looped and nubby yarns, and yarns that are spun with unlike materials (for instance wool and plastic), are especially susceptible. The constant dragging of the materials as they are drawn between the rows tears at the loose and fragile material and causes it to become ragged. The result can be a sad looking basket. There are several solutions to eliminate most of this problem.

If short lengths of a yard (meter) or less are used, the damage is minimal. The longer the strand, the more the problem seems to compound. Some fragile yarns cannot be used in coiling, but are acceptable in twining. Do not use fragile yarns in pierced weaves. If you are not sure whether a yarn will survive, drag your fingernails across it to test for tearing or make a small sample piece.

Handspuns that are loosely spun do not survive very well in coiling. Fine handspuns, however, can be overtwisted and doubled to strengthen and make them more durable using the following method. Cut off more than double the length you plan to use. Holding onto each end, twist the yarn until it kinks. Fold it in half without releasing the ends and the material will twist around itself. You now have a two-ply yarn that is stronger and will withstand more punishment than the original strand.

If the yarns become frayed in use, a little glue at the end of the material will keep the ends in place. Some yarns will take more glue than others. You will have to experiment with each type of yarn to find out how much is needed. Try to use as little glue as possible, especially white glue. Be sure to let the glue dry before wrapping the lengths into the ball. The glued ends will not show as they will be covered by succeeding wraps.

Nubby, rough textured yarns will work well in twining and fairly well in coiling except for pierced weaves.

If any of these materials seem to break very easily when pulling through and tightening, double or triple the yarn to make a stronger strand. Mohair comes in several weights. Use more than one strand of the lighter weights.

GENERAL INFORMATION ABOUT CORES

The core size determines the size of wrap that should be used, because the core is the dominant member of the basket. Small cores must be wrapped with thin wraps. Heavy wrap on small cores will make a soft spongy basket because the wrap is difficult to get tight and it does not allow the core to keep a straight line while wrapping.

Large cores, on the other hand, will accept any size wrap. The fastening back might be a little weaker with a thin wrap, but the fastenings occur so often that this balances out. Very thin wrap will make a smooth looking basket with a large core. If the basket seems to go very slowly when using thin wrap on large cores, double or triple the wrap. This will cover more area quickly, will make the material stronger, and will equalize the heavy look of the core.

Heavy wraps on large-cored baskets will give a big, strong look to the baskets. Anything that can be done in a small basket with a small core can be done in a large basket with a large core. It is only a difference in scale. The work is more difficult to achieve on a large core due to the difference in size, weight, and flexibility of the core material.

Large cores are difficult to find. If you desire a larger core, you can use several smaller cores together. Any core materials can be used together, but the softer the material used on the surface of the core group, the smoother the surface of the basket. Row shaping with a multiple core is simple. The individual units can be moved to allow the shape of the row to be round, oval, asymmetrical, or flat. The separate units can be divided and used for intricate decorative portions of the basket or edgings. These units can remain apart or be rejoined.

TAPERING WARPS AND CORES

Tapering the material in warps and cores is fairly simple except when using braided clothesline.

To taper a single-ply material, flatten the rope out and cut off at an angle. If there is more than one ply, unply the rope and lay the plys flat. Cut off each ply at an angle and re-ply the rope.

When tapering braided clothesline, the tapered end can break off if not treated properly. The material inside the braiding is usually a soft, short-fibered material that is easily broken up, and the braiding is fragile when cut at an angle. There are two ways to handle braided clothesline. You can paint the outside of the line with glue the length of the taper and allow to dry. Then cut the line at the desired angle. Or, if the filler is plyed material, do not glue the outside of the braiding. Instead, roll back the braided covering and unply the material, being very careful as it is fragile. Cut the taper and re-ply. Then roll the braided material back into place.

In tapering fiber rush, untwist the paper and lay it flat. Cut at an angle and twist back into place. In tapering reed, cut at an angle with a sharp knife or blade.

When cutting off a piece of core from the ball or reel, it is a good practice to cut it at an angle because more angle cuts are used than straight cuts.

SPLICING WARPS AND CORES

The general procedure for splicing is to taper the end of each piece of material to be spliced together. Glue the tapered edges with textile or white glue and hold together until set.

The glue has a dual purpose. It holds the ends together until they can be wrapped (the wrapping is the true fastening over the splice), as they can become a problem when wrapping over a splice area, especially if the core is fibrous. And the glue helps to keep the splice area under control.

When splicing reed the glue again becomes a third hand, making the splice easier to control. Hold the pieces together tightly while weaving over the splice, as the splice can break due to the stiffness of the core material. Here again the wrapping is the true fastening. If the glue does not seem to hold, use a tiny piece of masking tape over the separation.

Do not splice material that is going to show. It will not be attractive and the area will be weak. With open weaving, use sufficient length to finish the piece without splicing, or use materials which do not need to be spliced (pine needles, small reeds, etc.). These materials can be placed together in groups, and the new added ends are placed at irregular intervals and tucked into the bundle of existing pieces. This allows the ends to be hidden in the group.

When weaving over a splice, weave a little tighter to keep the splice from showing as a lumpy area. This is especially true in twining. When splicing ends in twining, try not to have all the splices occur in a line. Staggering will eliminate any heavy look if the splices are a little thick.

FIBER CHARACTERISTICS AND LONGEVITY

How the product you are planning to make will be used influences the materials chosen. Are you making samples, experimenting, or creating an art form? If you are making samples or experimenting, you should choose a material that is inexpensive and workable. If you are creating a piece for sale or exhibition, you should choose the proper materials to insure good craftsmanship and the longevity of the piece.

Warp and core materials, such as reeds, have proven themselves over the centuries as long lasting. Sisal, manila, and other similar rope products will survive very well when not subjected to water or chemicals. Synthetics and plastics are seemingly indestructible.

Jute on the other hand is more destructible. Exposed to the air, it begins to break down in a few years. Jute has the amazing property of responding to temperature and humidity. In dry conditions, it contains about .06% moisture, but in damp air, such as summer humidity or air-conditioned buildings, it absorbs up to .23%. This softens weak work made from jute and allows it to sag under its own weight, especially pieces with heavy extensions. When dried out again, the piece returns to the proper position. Softening is slight if the core is tightly wrapped because tight wrapping keeps the work firmer and allows less movement.

Living in a damp locale near the beach makes rust a problem. Recently, a steel armature that had been tightly wrapped for 8 years was dismantled. The steel was still highly polished, while similar bare rings left in the same room for a much shorter period were rusted. If jute is protected from the air by tight wraps it can last for many years. Only time will tell.

Wefts and wraps should be scrutinized as well. Linen, cotton, wool, and silk all have staying powers, as do all of the other animal fibers. Linen has the strongest properties of the plant fibers. Any materials will break down and rot if subjected to strong chemicals or water. Commercial animal fibers are mothproofed, but make sure that handspuns have been treated. Synthetics are strong materials and long lasting, except some rayon fibers.

Check your materials out before using them in a piece for sale or exhibition. If any materials are used which are of questionable longevity, make this known.

Wheels. 13" x 10" diameter (33.02cm x 25.40cm). Many little coiled starts in figure-eight weave are placed on a large coiled base to make an interesting basketform. The wheels are ornamented with rya and gold painted wooden beads. The material is a green gold synthetic rug yarn over jute.

Plaiting and Twining

3

Plaiting and twining are very similar in technique. Forerunners of textile weaving, they both contain a warp and a weft. They both also afford a slightly rounded bottom to a piece, which gives it a light, floating quality. Both techniques as covered in this book contain only two crossing elements. Simplicity of element and design rather than complexity of technique is the keynote.

The major difference between plaiting and twining is in the weft elements. Weft materials in plaiting move in straight lines crossing the warp materials in a perpendicular fashion. Any bending of the materials is done in the general shaping of the piece. The preferred material is flat and ribbonlike.

Twining requires a weft material that can be twisted and bent easily in any direction around heavy warps. The weft material usually totally covers the warp, and therefore it must be quite narrow and flexible, and is often cylindrical in shape. The flat, smooth look of plaiting contrasts sharply with the ribbed look of twining.

The materials used in both warp and weft are the major determination in the rigidity of the work. Both techniques, but especially plaiting, develop less support in the weaving process than coiling (see Chapter 4). Therefore the warp and weft materials must be chosen with the degree of firmness desired in the final product in mind.

Traditionally, throughout the world, cylindrical material (such as rattan or osier) is woven using a combination of plaiting and twining techniques into baskets, furniture, and many other practical items. This combination of methods will not be discussed further in this book, because the traditional materials that work best for it are specialized as to locale and therefore are not universally available. Plastic tubing and clothesline will work for this technique, but the resultant basket is not as strong as one made of natural materials, and the ends are difficult to disguise. Many good books are available to aid the craftsman wanting to make this type of basket.

PLAITING

In plaiting, the feeling is fluid and light. The work has movement because the construction allows freedom within the piece.

Plaiting weaves are: plain, check, diagonal, doubled plain, and twill. Different textures and materials make these weaves interesting and exciting. The more complicated plaited weaves are not included in this book because they are better served by using natural materials.

Over time the traditional plaiting technique used for baskets evolved into a technique for making fabric; therefore the terms used for plaiting are weaving terms. The vertical elements are called warps, and the horizontal elements are called wefts. As the basket sides begin to rise from the base or center, the wefts as well as the warps of the basket center become warps, and new strips are added as wefts. The weft piece being woven into the basket is called the weaver.

Plain Weave. This is the simple intersection of one element over another. The weaving is simply over one, under one.

Check Weave. This is plain weave using one color for the warp and another for the weft. This gives the weave a different look.

Diagonal Weave. This is plain plaiting turned diagonally to the shape of the basket after the center is woven and before weaving the sides (see Weaving the Sides of a Diagonal Basket). Check plaiting makes an interesting diagonal plaited basket.

DOUBLED VARIATIONS OF THE PLAIN WEAVE

These are two methods of changing plain plaiting for added effect. The first involves carrying two warps at a time in the weave, and the second carries two warps over two wefts at a time.

Method 1. The Single Row Variation Using Two Warps. Weave over two warps at a time alternating the weave in each row.

Method 2. The Double Row Variation Using Two Warps. Weave over two warps at a time for two rows before alternating. This gives a block effect to the weave.

Twill Weave. This is usually woven over two warps at a time. The pattern moves over one warp in each new row making a diagonal stairstep pattern across the basket. This pattern can move to the right or the left (as shown in the demonstration) and back and forth.

Twill can be used to make several variations of the diamond pattern. The pattern can vary from a straight over two and under two to as high as over three or four. Graph paper can be a great help in planning designs such as the diamond. Use one square on the paper to indicate one warp wide and one weft high.

Using one color in twill weave will give a textural look, while adding another color will add contrast and give a damask effect.

THE WORKING BOARD

When using contemporary materials like leather, plastic, or braids, the material has a tendency to slip. Pieces must be anchored down to keep them in place. Use a heavy piece of cardboard, Styrofoam,© a *hard* flat pillow or Celotex board as a pinning base. Do not stick the pins through

Plain Weave. A pattern of over one, under one every row.

Check Weave. Uses the plain weave with two colors.

Doubled Variation of the Plain Weave, Method 1. Weaves over two warps at a time every row.

Doubled Variation of the Plain Weave, Method 2. This variation weaves over two warps at a time for two rows before alternating to the opposite weave.

41

Right Diagonal Twill Weave. The direction of the steps moves right.

Left Diagonal Twill Weave. The direction of the steps moves left.

Zigzag Diagonal Twill Weave. The direction of the steps moves back and forth. The zigzags can be short or long.

Diamond Pattern in Twill Weave. The diamond pattern uses twill plaiting to create shapes. The weaving alters the over two, under two whenever necessary to create the desired pattern.

the material unless the holes will not show. Leather and plastics cannot be pinned, although braids and fabrics can. Directions in plaiting are primarily for leather because it is the material most available.

MEASURING MATERIAL

Strips of material for a basket need to be long enough to cover the entire center, reach up both sides, and finish the edges. Since the pieces lie tightly together in the weaving, the width of the pieces will determine the size of the basket. For instance, for a basket 4" x 4" x 4" (10.16 x 10.16 x 10.16cm), using ¼" (6.35mm) material, you will need 32 strips 12" (30.48cm) long, plus edges.

A square basket will require pieces all the same length, but a rectangular basket must allow for extra length one way and extra pieces the other. More lightweight materials will be needed if materials of different weights are used in the same basket. Weaving small sample pieces helps to determine how much material will be needed. The length of the side wefts for a straight-sided basket is the total length of all four sides plus the width of four warp strips. For a 4" x 4" x 4" (10.16 x 10.16 x 10.16cm) basket using ¼" (6.35mm) strips, you will need 16 to 17 strips, each 17" (43.18cm) long.

A diagonal basket does not need any strips other than those measured for the basket center because when the center is turned diagonally, the warps crisscross each other and become the wefts as well as the warps for the sides. To find the measurement of the strips for a diagonal basket, decide the distance the center of the basket will be from corner to corner and multiply that distance by 3. Then add enough to finish the edges as desired. The corners of the basket center are situated at the center point of the woven sides (see Weaving the Sides of the Diagonal Basket).

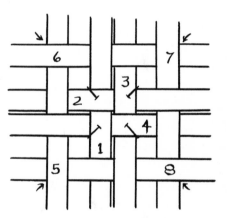

Starting a Basket Center. Weave four warp strips as shown. Beat them together and pin at the corners. Weave the next four warp strips as shown. Beat together and pin at the corners and along sides if needed. Continue weaving in this manner for the basket center.

STARTING A BASKET CENTER

This center will apply to all weaves. The example uses plain weave, but the basic method applies to all by changing the weaves. Place the pieces on the working board face down. This allows the sides to be bent upward without turning the woven center over to do so.

Following the illustration, take four pieces of material. Lay 1 on the working board vertically with the center of the strip near the center of the board. Now lay 2 across 1 horizontally with the lower edge of 2 at the center line. Lay 3 over 2 parallel to 1. Last, place 4 parallel to 2, weaving it over 3 and under 1. Beat or push the strips together with the fingers until the sides touch. Place pins at the outside corners of the weaving next to the strips.

Now weave 5 under 4 and over 2. Weave 6 over 5, under 1 and over 3. Next weave 7 over 6, under 2 and over 4. Last, weave 8 over 7, under 3, over 1, and under 5. Beat in with the fingers and move the pins to the outside corners. Add pins in other places around the edges if needed to hold in place. Keep adding weavers in groups of four until the planned size of the basket center is reached.

To keep the sides even in a rectangular basket, add the extra weavers evenly on both sides of the center.

MAKING THE FRAME

Since plaiting tends to move quite easily, a frame is a great help in controlling the basket shape. The frame forms a base on which the warps can be fastened. The frame gives tension to the side warps which helps during weaving and beating the wefts into place. A box or frame can be made by taping pieces of cardboard or popsicle sticks together in the desired size and shape. Since sizes will vary, one frame will not work for all plaited baskets, but the sections can be reused.

BENDING THE WARPS FOR THE SIDES

Thin flexible leather can conform to any angle desired or it can bend from a rounded bottom edge to a straight wall to form cylindrical basket sides. Heavy leather will not make an angled edge unless properly prepared. The back of the leather must be skived (trimmed away).

Bending the Warps for the Sides, Step 1. Cut through the leather part way.

Step 1. To do this use a very sharp blade to carefully cut through the back of the leather strip about one third to one half the depth at the fold line.

Step 2. Place the glue in the V-shaped incision and bend the leather to create the proper angle.

Step 2. Then hold the blade at an angle to the leather and cut toward the incision carefully from each side to trim away the edges. This leaves a V-shaped incision across the back of the strip. Lay glue in this incision and press the strip together at the angle desired. This will create a good bond. Place on the prepared frame to allow the glue to dry.

Plastic strips can be creased with an iron. Be sure to test the material for heat saturation before working into a basket. Too low heat only softens the plastic while too high heat can melt it. Be sure to protect your iron from melting plastic.

FASTENING WARPS TO THE FRAME

Place the frame on top of the woven center. Hold it in place while lifting and fastening the strips at the top edge with:

1. A very strong rubber band.

2. A strong piece of yarn or cord.

3. Cloth or masking tape.

4. A bulldog or binder clip.

5. A wing nut clamp described in Chapter 1.

WEAVING THE BASKET SIDES

The warps and wefts of the center become the warps for the basket sides. Be sure the warp strips are tightened into place before and during the weaving process.

SPLICING WEFTS FOR PLAITED BASKETS

Unless the weft material will adhere to itself, as natural leaf materials do, gluing will be necessary to splice the wefts. Make all the splices on one side of the basket.

Step 1. Choose a weaver. Weave the first row starting near the center of one side of the basket. Work around the basket leaving the last two warps unwoven. Leave both ends of the weaver extending over these warps.

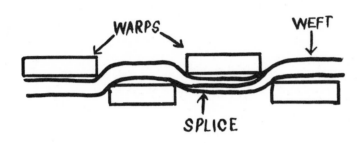

Splicing Wefts for Plaited Baskets, Step 1. Skive the backs of the strip ends at an angle.

Step 2. Glue the facing surfaces.

Step 3. Place the splice behind a warp. Press ends together and hold or clamp until dry.

To eliminate thickened splices, skive off the backs of the extending tips.

Step 2. Glue the facing surfaces of the weaver ends.

Step 3. Weave the ends into place making sure the splice is hidden under the warp. Tighten the row and press the ends together. Hold or clamp until dry.

Weave several rows before beating down. The top row of weaving will release and slip up a little each time, so weave the rows in groups before beating down. Continue weaving to the top of the basket.

WEAVING THE SIDES OF A DIAGONAL BASKET

A diagonally woven basket is not much more difficult to complete than a straight-sided basket and it affords a pleasing, different result.

Step 1. Place the frame diagonally on the basket center with the corners of the frame at the side center points. Bring up the woven corners and fasten them at the center points of the frame sides with a clip or clothespin.

Step 2. Starting at the bottom of one of the frame corners, pick up the weaver 1 on the left side and weave it along the right woven edge of the corner.

Step 3. Now pick up weaver 2 on the right side and weave it along the left woven edge of the corner and fasten in place as before. Continue alternating with each weaver left and right of the corner until the top of the corner is reached and all of the weavers have been woven in. Fasten in place securely and weave the other corners in the same way. Leave the clamps in place on the basket, but remove the frame.

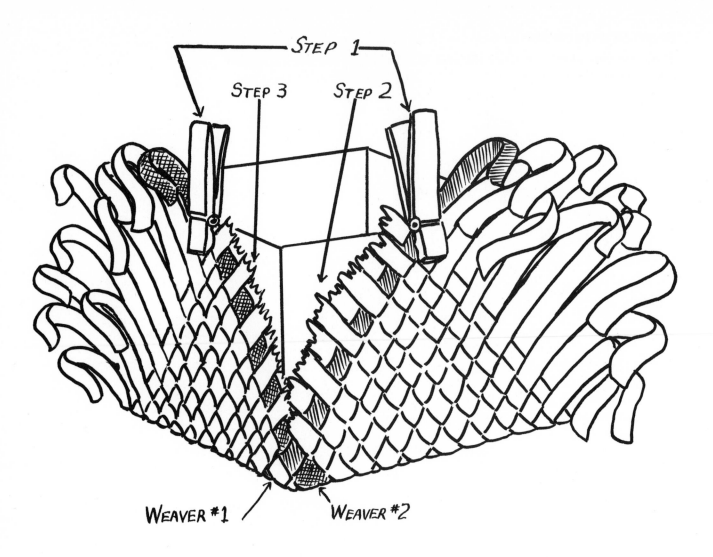

Weaving the Sides of the Diagonal Basket, Step 1. Bring up the corners of the woven center and clamp at the frame center points.

Step 2. Weave across the right side of the corner with weaver #1.

Step 3. Weave across the left side of the corner with weaver #2. Alternate sides to the top.

COMPLETING THE EDGES

There are two ways to prepare the edge of a basket for the finishing process. The edge can be trimmed off or it can be folded and rewoven.

The Trimmed Edge. Use this basket edge when more materials are to be added for strength. Use it for all types of materials and all kinds of plaiting, including diagonal plaiting.

Glue the weft and warp ends together along the edge and allow to set. Trim away the excess. The basket is now ready to add any finishes desired.

The Folded Edge. This edge is not as strong as one with added material, but it is neat and smooth. Use this edge when you are planning to make a lid for the basket, because it allows the lid to slip on easily. If you plan to use this edge for a simple basket without a lid, be sure the basket is very lightweight. A heavy basket needs a stronger edge.

For plain plaited baskets, allow for an extra row of weft. Glue the extra weft row and the warp ends as above and allow to set. Fold down the extra row inside the basket and reweave the warp ends into the basket. Trim off any exposed ends.

For diagonal plaited baskets, fold the edge at the line and reweave the ends on the inside of the basket. Trim off ends.

If decoration is desired, it may be added around the edge of the basket. If the basket is to have a lid, add the decoration below the line of the lid. The decoration can be matched to that on the lid.

Using an Orange Stick as a Reweaving Tool. It can be difficult to weave the warp ends back into the inside of the basket without a tool. An orange stick is a very good aid in reweaving. Choose one with a flat end.

Step 1. Fold the warp end placing the fold slightly below the edge of the weft row. Slip the orange stick under the weft and pull the weft away. Push the warp fold into the pocket.

Step 2. Put the orange stick into the warp fold and push it under the weft and smooth out. Trim off the excess warp end below the weft. The warps can be glued, but this is not necessary.

STRENGTHENING THE EDGE

Since the edge of the basket is the part most handled, it must be the strongest. Unfortunately, it is the weakest part, therefore it must be strengthened.

A single weft strip can be placed either inside or outside of and parallel to the basket edge over the last weft row. The ends should be skived, glued, and spliced. This weft row can be touched on the back with glue several times in order to fasten it temporarily in place along the edge until it can be permanently fastened down.

Two strips can be added to the basket both inside and out, or one extra wide strip, which will fold over the edge and cover both sides the width of the first weft row can be used.

If leather is used for the extra strips, the cut edges may be stained with leather stain to disguise them before fastening to the basket.

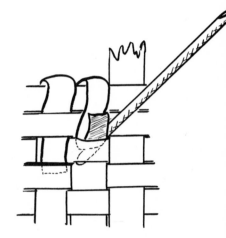

Using an Orange Stick as a Reweaving Tool, Step 1. Pull out the weft until the folded warp can be slipped beneath it.

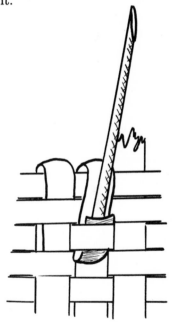

Step 2. Push the warp strip through the weft opening with the stick.

Adding Decorative Knots —
the Overhand Knot. The overhand knot is a simple tie made
in a strand of material as
shown.

Single Wrap Finish. Pierce
holes at ¼" (.64cm) intervals
or more beneath the edge strip
with a sharp tool. Make sure
they are large enough to allow
the needle and lacing to pass.
Overcast the edges entering
the holes from the front.
Glue and conceal the ends between the edge strips and the
basket.

Double Wrap Finish. Pierce
the holes twice as far apart as
the single wrap. Follow directions for single wrap to the
end of the row. Reverse direction and rewrap using the
same holes making sure the
wraps cross at the top edge of
the basket.

ADDING DECORATIVE KNOTS

Choose the lacing for decorative knots from such material as leather
lacing, heavy linen cord, or attractive round braids. Make holes with a
piercing tool through the basket at the center of each warp end making
sure they are centered on the extra strip. Make the holes large enough to
allow the threaded needle and lacing material to pass.

Measure the amount of lacing needed to tie a single or double overhand
knot. Multiply the amount needed to make the knot by the number of
punched holes and add the basket circumference. Add 12" (30.48cm) or
more for extra working length.

Glue the end of the lacing and place it between the extra strip and the
basket, press together, and let set. Needle through the first hole. Tie the
overhand knot carefully so it lies tightly against the surface of the basket
and will not pull back through the hole. Now needle back through the
hole, and continue the row in the same way. If using two-sided material
like leather lacing, make sure the surface of the material shows in the
knot. Needle between the extra strip and the basket after the last hole,
glue the lacing, and pull through. Hold until set, then cut off the end.

Adding Bells and Beads. Measure two times the circumference of the
basket and cut a corresponding length of lacing. Punch holes around the
edge and fasten the end of the lacing as above. Thread the lacing onto a
tapestry needle, needle through the first hole from inside the basket, and
pull through. Thread a bell or bead onto the lacing and needle back
through the same hole. Pull tight. Continue to add bells or beads throughout the row. Finish off as above.

TRADITIONAL FINISHES WITH A NEW TWIST

Traditionally, to finish off a basket, rigid strips of material are placed
around both sides of the edge and flexible strips of material are wrapped
around them and through the top of the basket in several ways.

WRAPPED FINISHES

This finish is begun by following the directions given above for strengthen-
ing the edge of the basket by adding strips. The lacing material should
blend with the basket material. If a contrasting material is used, make sure
the color and the type of edge finish chosen do not detract from the
basket.

Single Wrap. Punch evenly spaced holes through the warps below the
added strips at no less than ¼" (6.35mm) intervals, including the spaces
between the warps as holes. Measure the length needed to wrap around
the strips from the first to the second hole. Multiply this length by the
number of holes in the basket. Add some extra working length. Fasten
the end of the lacing under the inside strip with glue and let set. Thread
the lacing on to a tapestry needle. Overcast the lacing around the edge,
needling through the holes from the outside of the basket. Do not let flat
lacing material twist. Finish off by fastening the lacing under the extra
strip inside the basket with glue. Trim off the end.

Double Wrap. Punch holes in the same way as the single wrap at no less
than ½" (12.7mm) intervals. After wrapping the edge with the single
wrap, turn and wrap in the opposite direction needling through the same

holes. Make sure the second wrap crosses the first wrap at the top edge. Finish off in the same way as the single wrap.

FEATHERSTITCH BRAIDING

Punch holes at ¼" (6.35mm) intervals. These holes may be placed in a straight line at the base of the added strip or staggered alternately below and in the center of the strip. Be sure the hole is large enough to allow the needle and lacing to pass through easily. Use a needle with as slim an eye as possible.

The amount of lacing required is determined by the number of holes and the type of material. Make a sample sequence, remove, and measure the length. Make sure there is enough to finish the lacing without splicing. Allow extra length for working.

Step 1. Thread the lacing on the needle, glue the end of the lacing, and place it between the strip and the basket. Allow to set. Needle through the first hole from the front and leave a loop.

Step 2. Needle between the lacing and the top of the basket and pull through without twisting, leaving a small loop.

Step 3. Now needle through the loop and pull the lacing through without twisting, leaving another loop.

Step 4. Pull the first and second loops tight. Pull the third loop tight.

Step 5. Repeat this braid sequence around the top of the basket. After finishing the last sequence, needle through the first loop and pull the lacing through. Enlarge the first hole and needle through. Pull the lacing through and slip the needle under the lacings inside the basket up close to the braiding for about ½" (12.7mm). Glue the lacing, pull through, and cut off.

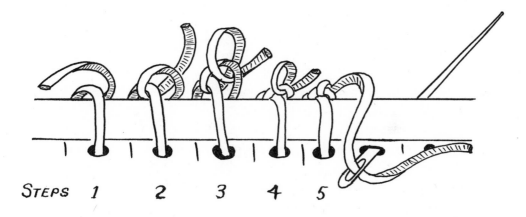

STEPS   1   2   3   4   5

Featherstitch Braiding Finish, Step 1. Needle through the first hole from the front, pull through leaving a loop.

Step 2. Needle through the loop without twisting material leaving another loop.

Step 3. Needle through the second loop without twisting the material leaving another loop.

Step 4. Tighten the first and second loops.

Step 5. Tighten the third loop and needle through the next hole.

MAKING A LID

The lid is made in the same way as the basket itself, except that the lid often has decorative elements in the center, and it needs to be slightly larger than the basket to slip over the basket edge easily. The decorative elements are put on before the edge is finished off. Leave the basket on the frame while adding the decoration to make working easier. See Chapter 5 for imbricated weaves that can be used as lid decoration in plaiting.

Adding Bells or Beads. Place the object on the lid in position. Thread a strip of weaving material through the object and weave each end through the adjacent rows on the lid to the edges. If the object has a small hole, punch two holes through the strip of weaving material and tie the object onto it with waxed linen. Now weave the strip into place. The extra ends will be included in the edge finishing. Remember there must be an uneven number of rows on the lid to allow a single object to be placed in the center of the lid if it is to be woven in place.

Adding a Handle. Make a coil of rigid material and weave the ends into the selected woven rows as above. A ring can be wrapped with flexible material and attached to the lid with the wrapping material in the same way.

The fastening material for any decorative object can be the material used in the basket or a contrasting material that can be included in the lid design.

TWINING

Two things are added in twining: a twist and another strand of weft. The twist in the wefts gives more strength and requires less rigid materials. Any type of material that will satisfy the desired end result can be used for the warps regardless of look. Since twining requires a beating process to force the elements together, fibrous materials like jute make poor warps. The fibers become dislodged and work to the surface of the basket. Plastic or braided clothesline work well. Beating is done with the fingers, a tapered popsicle stick, an orange stick, or a heavy tapestry needle.

Twining weaves are plain (single and double), twill, and wrap. Similar in appearance to plaiting, they allow more freedom in pattern and design. Twining is worked with two strands of weft at the same time. The two strands of material are twisted together as they are woven across the row. The twists are either a half or a full twist. Each warp is covered back and front in the same weaving operation.

The half twist is the more common of the two techniques. A simple crossover, it is used to create a vertical stripe. An uneven number of warps will produce a checked look with two colors (see the illustration of weaves and color patterns later in this chapter).

The full twist is used when a definite pattern or design is planned for the basket surface. The desired color can be brought to the surface when needed.

TWINING WITH THE HALF TWIST

When working on the body of the basket, the work progresses in one direction. At the basket base or center, separate units or straps are twined independently and then joined to make the body of the basket. When working on the center straps, it is necessary to weave back and forth.

Plain Twine. Uses one warp.

Diamond Pattern. Alters the use of two warps in the twill weave when needed to create the pattern.

Left Diagonal Twill. Moves the two warp pattern over one warp to the left each row to create the pattern.

Zigzag Twill Weave. Uses the left and right diagonal twill weaves moving back and forth the desired number of times.

Right Diagonal. Uses the twill twine moving over one warp to the right each row.

Checked Plain Twine. Uses the half twist with two colors.

Broken Vertical Stripe. Made in the same way as checked plain twine, except a full twist is used at the beginning of the row to control the stripe.

Loop variations (left and right strap). The placement of the loops can be varied as well as the color used.

Method 1 (below) is the preferred direction and is used throughout the basket unless the weaving direction is reversed. Method 2 is used to reverse direction when weaving the center straps or when a design is being developed separately (see Chapter 6). Method 2 retains the directional slant of method 1.

Method 1 (Moving toward the Working Hand Side). The weft strands are called A and B. Make butterflies at the end of each strand (see Chapter 2 for directions). Weave strand A under warp 1 and drop it down (Step 1). Pick up strand B and weave it over warp 1 and under warp 2 and drop it down (Step 2). Continue this sequence across the row or around the basket (Step 3).

Method 2 (Moving toward the Holding Hand Side). Weave A under warp 1 and place up (Step 1). Pick up B and weave over warp 1 and under warp 2 and place up (Step 2). Continue this sequence across the row (Step 3).

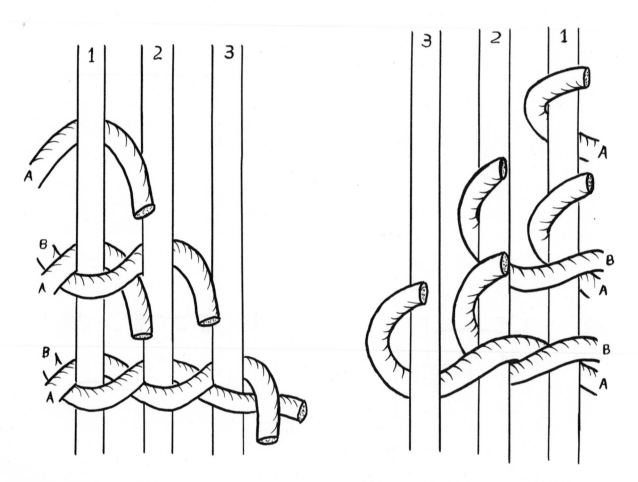

Twining with the Half Twist, Method 1, Step 1. Weave A under warp 1 and drop down.

Step 2. Weave B over warp 1 and under warp 2 and drop down.

Step 3. Alternate across the row or around the basket.

Twining with the Half Twist, Method 2, Step 1. Weave A under warp 1, and place up.

Step 2. Weave B over warp 1 and under warp 2, and place up.

Step 3. Continue this sequence across the row.

TWINING WITH THE FULL TWIST

While the strands in the half twist alternate front and back by crossing each other, the strands of the full twist never cross over to the other side of the warp. This allows two colors to be controlled when making designs.

Method 1 (Working toward the Working Hand Side). Weave A under warp 1 and drop it down (Step 1). Lay B across warp 1 (Step 2). Pick up A, wrap it around B, and weave it under warp 2 (Step 3). Hold B and pull on A until the twist is hidden under warp 2 (Step 4). Repeat this sequence across the color pattern.

Method 2 (Working toward the Holding Hand Side). Weave A under warp 1 and place up (Step 1). Lay B across warp 1 (Step 2). Wrap A around B and weave it under warp 2 (Step 3). Hold B and pull on A until the twist is hidden under warp 2 (Step 4). Repeat this sequence across the color pattern.

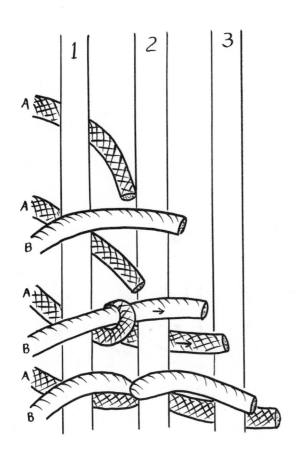 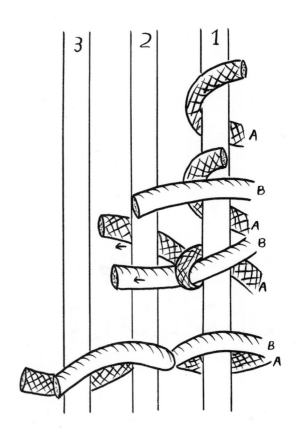

Twining with the Full Twist, Method 1, Step 1. Weave A under warp 1.

Step 2. Place B over warp 1.

Step 3. Wrap A around B, weave under warp 2.

Step 4. Hold B and pull A until the twist is hidden under warp 2.

Twining with the Full Twist, Method 2, Step 1. Weave A under warp 1 and place up.

Step 2. Place B across warp 1.

Step 3. Wrap A around B, weave under warp 2 as shown.

Step 4. Hold B and pull A until the twist is hidden under warp 2.

TWINING WEAVES

Three types of twining weaves are plain, twill, and wrap.

Plain Twining (Single and Double). This kind of twining can be woven over one warp (single) or two warps (double) at a time as in plaiting. The resultant pattern is respectively narrow or wide ribbing. Used for the basic weave of a basket, this is the best weave to use for basket centers as it is the strongest of the twining weaves. A pattern can be developed by using a different color for each strand.

Twill Twining. This is woven over two warps at a time as in plaiting to develop the pattern. In order to allow the pattern to work out naturally without having to use the full twist or alter the pattern at the end of the row, it is best to add an extra warp to keep the warp count odd. If new warps are added to enlarge the basket, keep the total count uneven.

The twined patterns are the same as the plaited twills: left and right diagonals, zigzag, and diamond. The change of direction of the pattern is achieved by using the full twist. When the end of each row is reached, adjustments will need to be made to develop the pattern. It is a good idea to make graph paper drawings of the proposed patterns until you can work them out in your head as you weave.

Wrap Twining. In this kind of twining a horizontal piece of warp is added either to the surface of the basket as a decorative element or to the inside for extra strength.

ADDING A HORIZONTAL WARP

Taper a piece of warp. Following the illustration, lay the warp on the surface of the basket with the tapered end extending about 1" (2.54cm) beyond the holding hand side of the working point. Make a half twist at the vertical warp, wrap the horizontal warp with the front strand the number of times needed to carry it to the next vertical warp. Make a half twist, weave around the vertical warp and make another half twist. Wrap the horizontal warp again with the front strand covering it up to the next vertical warp. Be sure to wrap the horizontal warp carefully to cover it completely. Continue around the basket in the same way until reaching a

Adding a Horizontal Warp. Make a half twist on the working hand side of the vertical warp. Place the taper of the horizontal warp in front of the vertical warp. Carry B around the horizontal warp the number of times needed to carry it to the next vertical warp. Half twist the strands, twine around the vertical warp and make another half twist.

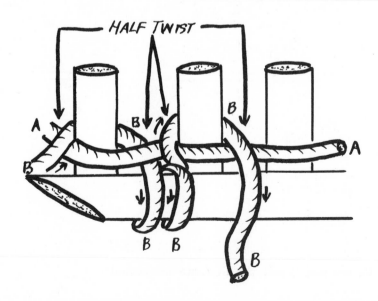

54

point about 1" (2.54cm) from the tip of the taper cut. Cut and splice the horizontal warp and finish the row.

When placing a horizontal warp inside the basket, follow the same directions except the horizontal warp is wrapped with the back strand.

ADDING NEW WEFTS

New weft strands are necessary when either weft strand gets short.

Step 1. Needle the new weft strand under the twining next to the holding hand side of the warp after passing over the front of the previous warp.

Step 2. Needle the new piece of weft which will replace it in the same space and weave this new weft behind the next warp.

Step 3. If the other weft is being replaced as well (for a color change), take the second strand in front of the next warp, needle down in the same way as the first strand, and cut off.

Step 4. The second strand is replaced in the same way as the first.

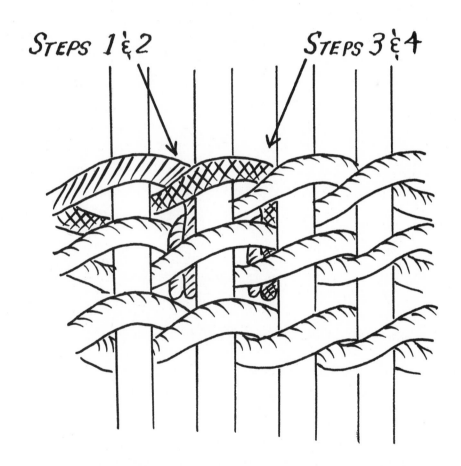

Adding New Wefts, Step 1. Needle the end of the weft down on the holding hand side of the warp.

Step 2. Needle the new wrap beside the old for 1" (2.54cm). Weave behind the next warp.

Step 3. Repeat step 1 with the alternate old strand.

Step 4. Repeat step 2 with the alternate new strand.

THE CENTER

Two methods are used for basket centers: cross warping and woven. Both methods work with groups of warps. The number of groups varies from two to six, and they can be handled in many ways. The number of warps to a group varies from three to eight.

One way to place the basket center warps is to think of the working board as a map. North-south is the vertical placement and east-west is horizontal.

CROSS WARPING

Cross warping is a simple technique for making the basket center.

Method 1 (Using Two Groups of Four). Measure the warps by adding the length of the center, both sides, and the amount needed to finish both edges.

Cut eight lengths of warp. Following the illustration, place the first group of four warps North-South on the working board, pinning them top and bottom. The pinning marks will not show because the weft covers the warps. Lay the second group East-West across the first at the center point. Mark each warp with a pen at the edge where the warp intersects the other group (see the dotted lines in illustration). The center straps will be twined between these markings on each group (see below).

Method 2 (Using Four Groups of Four). Cut 16 warps. Following the illustration, place the first group of warps in a Northwest-Southeast direction and pin in place. The second group is placed Northeast-Southwest, the third group East-West, and the last group North-South. Mark the intersecting edges with a pen (see dotted lines in illustration). Remove the pins from one end of the top three groups and lay these groups back out of the way.

Twine each group from the bottom markings to the top (see below) needling the ends down in all groups except the last (North-South). Leave the butterflies on the North-South group attached to the North working hand side (see arrow 1 in illustration).

Starting at arrow 2, weave around the center for two rows following the dotted line in the illustration. Remember to pull the warps into the spaces between the straps to even them. Now the center can be removed from the board.

There are many variations beyond this for cross warping groupings.

TWINING THE CENTER STRAPS

Measure about six arm lengths on a piece of weft. This single strand will become two strands after warp 1. Make butterflies at each end (see Chapter 2 for directions). The butterflies will be used as weavers.

Since twining, like plaiting, is a weaving operation, it is best done with the warps under tension at the outset. Remove the pins from one end of the East-West group and lay the warps back out of the way.

Starting at the bottom markings, weave one end of the weft strand under warp 1 (this is Step 1 of Half Twist, Method 1). Now the single strand becomes strands A and B. Pick up B, weave over warp 1 and under warp 2 and place down. Continue Method 1 to warp 4.

To reverse direction and begin with Method 2 you must half twist the

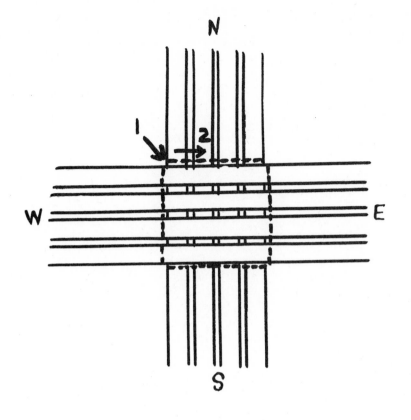

Cross Warping, Method 1.
Place the warps as shown, pin both ends, and mark the intersections. Unpin one end in the top group and lay aside. Twine from the bottom lines to the top markings. Half twist the strands around the last warp, needle down 1'' (2.54cm) and cut off. Lay the bottom group aside, and replace the top group. Twine the top group as before leaving the butterflies attached at arrow 1. Replace both groups in order. Twine along dotted lines starting at arrow 2.

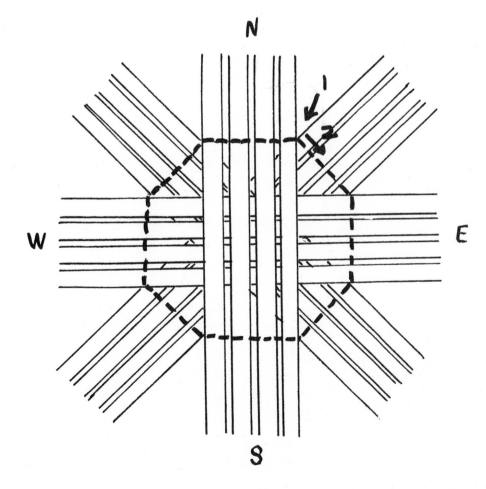

Cross Warping, Method 2.
Place the groups starting with the northeast-southwest group. Pin in place and mark the warps. Unpin one end and lay top groups aside. Twine each group as in method 1, leaving only the top butterflies attached at arrow 1. Replace the groups and pin down. Twine in method 1 for two rows along dotted lines starting at arrow 2.

N

Woven Center, Method 1.
Place the bottom triangle
weaving the group together
as shown. Pin in place. Place
and pin the top triangle, and
mark the edges as shown. Remove the pins from one end of
the top five groups and lay
aside. Twine each of the
groups as in cross warping,
leaving the butterflies attached
to the top group at arrow 1.
Replace and reweave the triangles and pin in place. Twine
two rows along the dotted
lines starting at arrow 2.

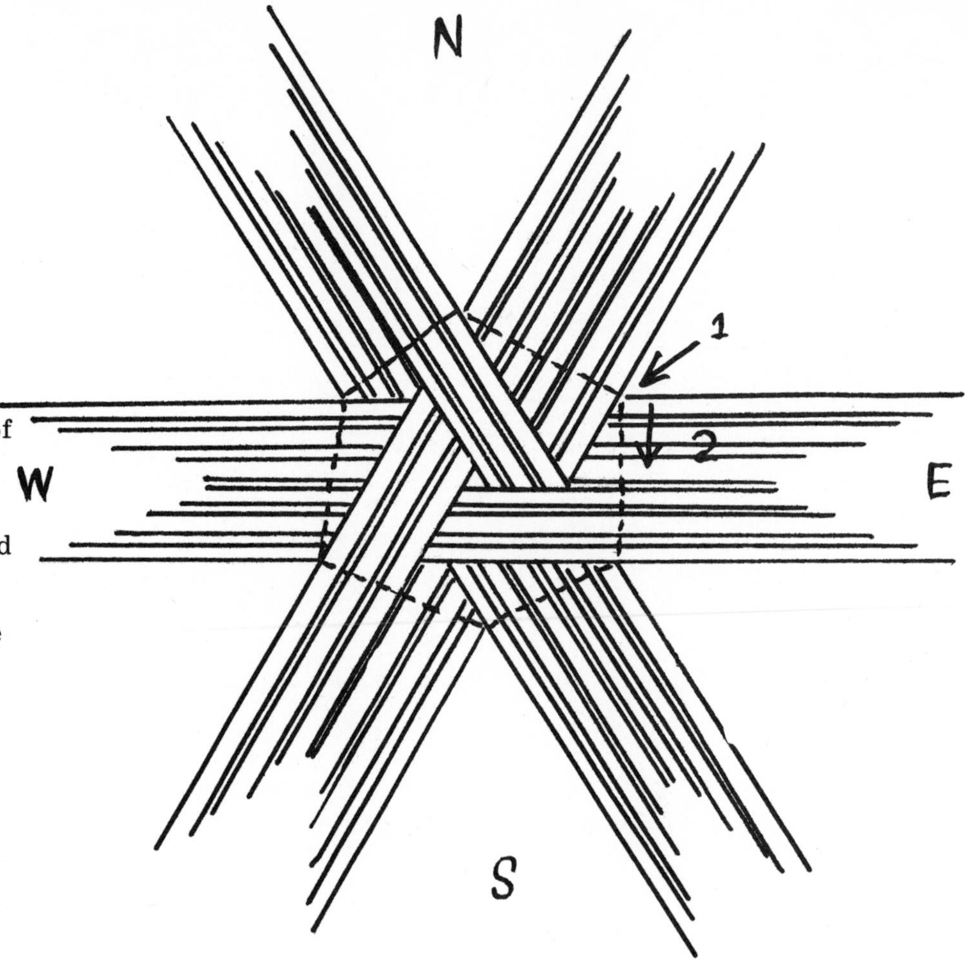

W   E

S

N

Woven Center, Method 2.
Place the warp groups on the
board weaving them together
as shown. Mark the intersections. Twine each group separately leaving the butterflies
attached only to the top group
at arrow 1. Replace the
groups. Twine for two rows
starting at arrow 2 along the
dotted lines.

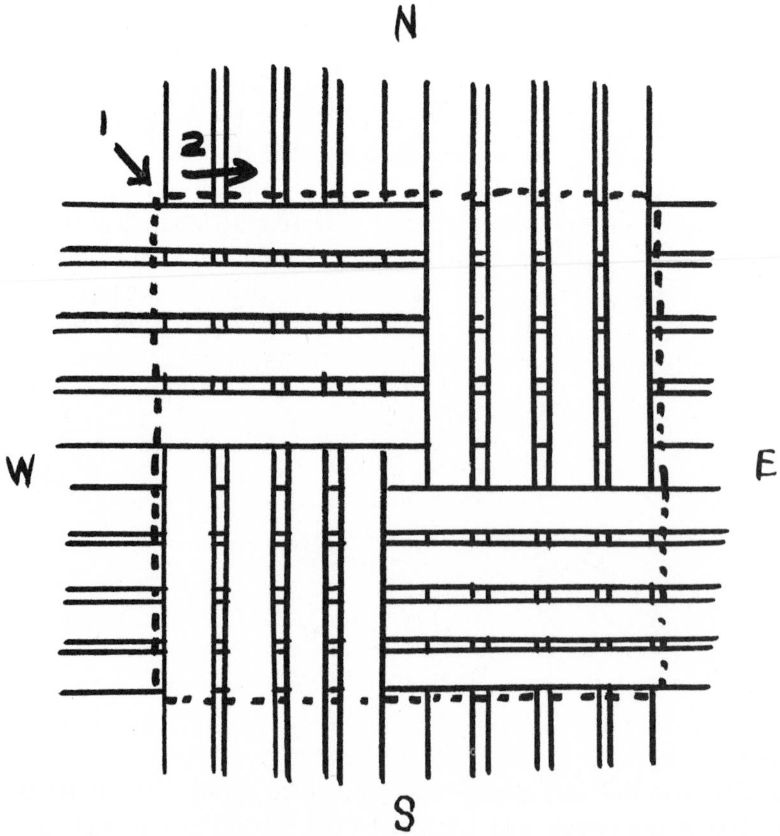

W   E

S

end. Leave B down and pick up A. Weave A under warp 4 and place it up. Pick up B and weave over warp 4 and under warp 3 and place it up. Continue Method 2 across to warp 1 and place B up.

To half twist this end, weave A back under warp 1 and place it down. Now you are ready to start back with Method 1 again.

Continue weaving the strap back and forth in this way. Beat the weaving together tightly so none of the warp shows and it is firm to the touch. When you reach the top markings, half twist the strands and needle down 1" (2.54cm) and cut off. Unpin one end and lay back.

Pin the East-West group back in place. Turn the board, placing the working hand side down. Twine this group in the same way ending with the butterflies attached to the working hand side. Turn the board back to the original position which now places the butterflies on the North holding hand side (see arrow 1 in illustration for Method 1).

Replace the two groups in their proper positions. Pick up the butterflies and weave from arrow 2 around the basket center following the dotted line in the illustration. Weave two rows in this manner. As you work, pull the warps toward the corner spaces. After this the center is fastened together and can be removed from the board to finish the basket.

WOVEN CENTERS

Woven basket centers are especially exciting in twining for their appearance of movement. They are beautiful in wall hangings. Below are two examples.

Method 1 (Using Six Groups of Three). This center made in two triangular groupings has a very unusual look. When placed together, the two triangles become a six-pointed star. As in cross warping, the numbers can vary in the groups as long as the numbers in each group are the same.

Cut 18 warps. Following the illustration, lay the first group on the board East-West above the center point. Lay the second group across it Southwest-Northeast, and the third group Northwest-Southeast, weaving the warp pieces over the second group and under the first. Even up the legs of the triangle. Invert the second triangle placing the point up when pinning it over the first. Evenly space the triangles and mark the warps at the points where the groups meet. Mark straight lines across each group of warps from point to point (see the dotted lines in the illustration).

Remove the pins from one end of the top five groups and put them out of the way. Twine five groups and needle down the ends. Weave the top group and leave the butterflies attached to the North working hand side of the group (see arrow 1 in the illustration). Weave around the center for two rows using cross warping, Method 1, following the dotted lines in the illustration starting at arrow 2. Pull the end warps into the spaces to even them up. Remove the center from the board and begin weaving the basket.

Method 2 (Using Four Groups of Four). Cut 16 warps. Following the illustration, lay the first group North-South on the board on the holding hand side of center and pin in place. Lay the second group on top East-West above the center point. Lay the third group North-South parallel to the first group and over the second group at the working hand side of center. Weave the last group over the third group and under the first group below the center and parallel to the second group. Mark the warps at the intersecting edges (see dotted line in illustration).

Remove the end pins from one end of groups four, three, and two and lay out of the way. Weave each center strap as above and needle down the ends of the first three groups. Leave the attached butterflies on the last group at the North working hand side (see arrow 1 in the illustration). Weave around the center, starting at arrow 2, following the dotted lines in the illustration for two rows. Pull the edge warps into the spaces. Remove from the board to weave the basket.

To make a rectangular basket, add another group of four warps. Place it parallel to groups 1 and 3, making sure these groups are centered on the East-West groups. Group 5 would weave under group 2 and over group 4.

ADDING EXTRA WARPS

To enlarge the size of the basket, extra warps can be added. Taper the end of the warp and place it beside an existing warp. Weave as if these warps were one piece for 1" (2.54cm) before separating into two warps. Extra warps must be added evenly around the basket to keep the shaping even. If warp material has a filler, glue the taper to the existing warp to keep the filler inside. A little glue applied at the taper is handy to keep the extra warp from slipping out of position for the first few rows as well.

Be sure to weave two rows around the basket center before trying to add extra warps.

SHAPING THE BASKET

Shaping to increase the size, add new warps, or make the weave a little looser is easy in twining. However, do not loosen the weave too much or the basket will be weak. To decrease the size, tighten up on the twining or taper off the warps evenly and weave them into another warp. This latter procedure is essentially a reversal of adding new warps.

PREPARING THE EDGE

At the top of the basket needle one strand 1" (2.54cm) under the twining and cut off. The other strand will be used to fasten the edging to the basket.

Edgings are needed to strengthen the top of the basket, protect it, and decorate it. These include: straight or wrapped edge, looped or scalloped edge, and fringed edge.

Straight or Wrapped Edge, Method 1. Trim the warps off to ¼" (.64cm) around the top. Undo the butterflies. Needle one strand down and cut off. Thread the other on a needle. Lay the tapered warp on top of the basket above the remaining butterfly end. Overcast the edge with the weft entering the basket about ¼" (.64cm) into the twining. Keep the overcasting pushed together and tightly wrapped.

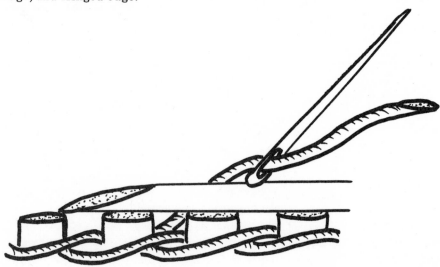

STRAIGHT, OR WRAPPED EDGE

This is the simplest edge technically and it provides a clean, strong top to the basket.

Cut off the ends of the warps to ¼" (6.35mm) above the twining. Place the remaining butterfly from the warp weaving on the inside of the basket edge. Taper the end of a piece of warp. Unwind the butterfly and thread on to a tapestry needle (blunt or sharp). As in the illustration, lay the extra warp on top of the warp ends with the end of the tapered cut above the threaded weft end.

Pierce the outside of the basket below the warp ends and about ¼" (6.35mm) into the twining. Pull through and tighten. Overcast or wrap the entire edge tightly, keeping the wraps close together to completely cover the edge warp. Pierce the basket evenly whether through warp or weft. If the warp is hard, like reed, pierce the warp with a sharp tool. If you do not want to go through the reed warp, pierce the basket between the warps the number of times needed to overcast the edge warp. Keep the wraps and needled areas smooth and even.

At 1" (2.54cm) before the taper cut, fasten with a clothespin. Cut off the warp and taper the end. Splice the warp ends and finish the edge in the same way. Needle under the twining for 1" (2.54cm), pull through, and cut off.

Alternatively, you can taper the ends of two pieces of warp. Place one piece inside and one outside the edge of the basket. Then follow the directions above, wrapping the edge and the two pieces of warp tightly, and finish off.

LOOPED AND SCALLOPED EDGES (Single, Double, and Triple)

The looped edge is simple but attractive for a twined basket. Each warp end is bent, inserted in, and attached to the first, second, or third warps. The illustration shows the three methods.

Bend one warp end to determine the proper length needed and trim away the excess from each warp end on the basket. Taper, glue, and insert the end into the warp space. Now it is ready to be wrapped. On double and triple loops, overlap the warps the same way each time.

The scalloped edge is very similar to the looped edge, except the loops are layered. They are wrapped in the same way. Attach the first row of warps to every second warp space in a single line. Attach the second row of warps on top of the first row to every second warp space in the same way.

Wrapping the Looped or Scalloped Edge. As in the wrapped edge, leave one of the butterflies attached to the basket edge. Thread the weft from the butterfly onto a tapestry needle.

Step 1. Needle down one strand and thread the other on a needle. Bend the first warp end around to the desired position and cut off excess. Cut all the warp ends the same length and taper. Glue, bend and insert into the proper space. Wrap the first loop tightly keeping the wraps pushed together.

Step 2. When you reach the next loop, wrap over both pieces of warp several times, not completely covering the warp until you reach the edge of the basket.

Wrapping the Looped or Scalloped Edges, Step 1. Wrap the nearest loop tightly and evenly, covering it well.

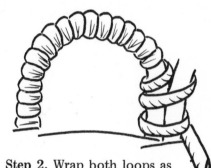

Step 2. Wrap both loops as one moving quickly to the base of the ends without covering them completely, as shown.

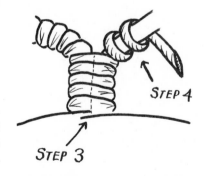

Step 3. Wrap up again tightly, covering the bases completely.

Step 4. At the separation point, wrap the next loop.

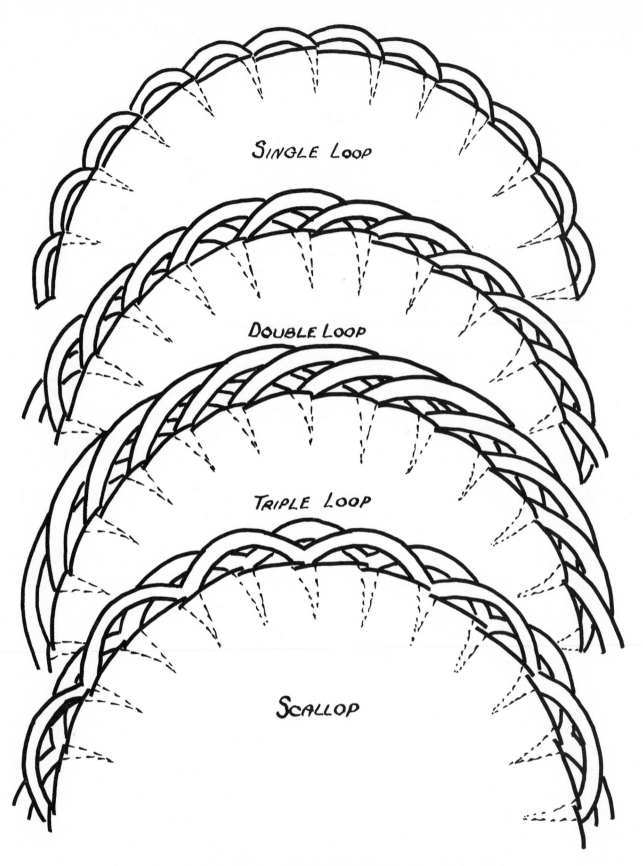

SINGLE LOOP

DOUBLE LOOP

TRIPLE LOOP

SCALLOP

Looped and Scalloped Edges for Twining. The beautiful looped edges make an attractive way to finish off the twined basket.

Step 3. Reverse direction and wrap carefully up the two pieces of warp again until they separate.

Step 4. Now wrap over the next loop as before.

Continue wrapping the loops until all are covered. You will find the wrapping direction changes with each loop. Needle under the twining 1" (2.54cm), pull through, and cut off.

Adding New Weft on the Loops. Here is the procedure to follow if you run out of wrapping weft.

Step 1. Lay the end on top of the warp loop; fasten with a clothespin.

Step 2. Needle the new piece of weft ½" to 1" (1.27 to 2.54cm) under the previous wrapping. Carefully pull the weft through until the end is hidden under the wrapping. Continue wrapping as before, covering the end of the old wrap that was laid on the warp.

FRINGED EDGES

These are two methods of fringing edges that require splicing.

Method 1. Cut the warps about 3" (7.62cm) from the end of the twining. Taper the ends. Following the splice directions in Chapter 2, layer 9" to 12" (22.9 x 30.5cm) weft pieces to make a taper of the weft and splice this onto the tapered warp end. Be sure to add enough weft pieces to make the tapered end and the added weft the same wrapped diameter as the warp.

Step 1. Thread a tapestry needle with three arm lengths of weft. Wrap each warp end tightly covering the splice making sure there is no lump at the splice point. Bring the wrapped warp down on to the basket surface below the basket edge forming a loop with the wrapped piece. Continue to wrap the extended warp and fasten it to the basket surface at the same time. Needle through to the inside of the basket, around the warp and back out at each wrap of the loop piece. Watch the inside of the basket to keep the work neat and even. A curved needle can be used to pierce the basket warp piece instead of encircling it, if desired.

Step 2. When the loop is securely fastened with 6 to 10 wraps or more, needle the wrapping weft under the twining 1" (2.54cm), pull through and cut off, leaving the fringe hanging. Repeat this process for every warp end in the basket, making sure the loops are even. Trim the fringe the length desired.

Method 2. Taper the ends of the warps 1" (2.54cm) below the planned edge of the basket. Splice weft materials to the tapered ends as in the first method. Finish twining the basket—tightening the splice area, keeping it smooth, even, and without lumps.

Needle the warp ends back into the next warp space (never its own) about ½" to 1" (1.27 to 2.54cm) and pull through (see illustration). Trim the warp fringe as desired for a decorative effect.

Fringed edges are especially attractive on handbags, tote bags, pillows, etc. If desired, a beautiful soft bag can be made using many strands of weft material as the warp. In this instance, the fringe does not need to be spliced.

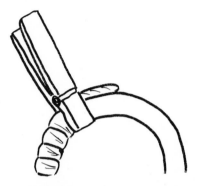

Adding New Weft on the Loops, Step 1. Lay the end of the weft on the loop, and fasten with a clothespin.

Step 2. Thread a new piece of weft on the needle, and needle under the previous wraps.

Fringed Edge, Method 1, Step 1. Splice weft material onto tapered warps about 3" (7.62cm) from basket edge using enough weft to duplicate the warp diameter.

Step 2. Wrap the extended warp ends and fasten each to the basket as shown in this side view.

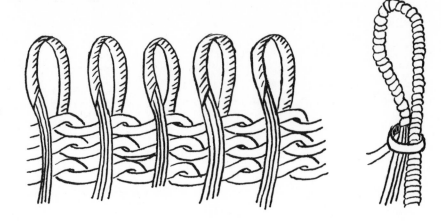

Fringed Edge, Method 2. Needle the ends of the multi-strand warps down in the spaces occupied by the next warps for about ½" to 1" (1.27cm to 2.54cm). Bring the ends to the basket surface as fringe.

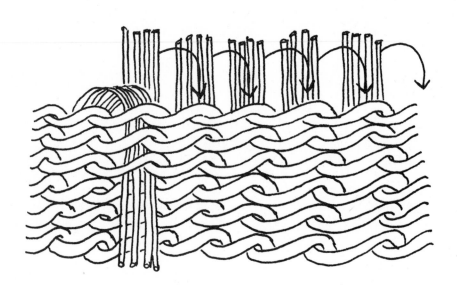

SAMPLE PROJECTS

An excellent way to learn weaves without having to develop each into a separate basket is by making a sample piece. It will give you an idea how each weave is made, and it will be something to which you can refer at a later time.

Narrow plaiting samples can be made that are long enough to complete the number of patterns you plan for the sample. The edges can be glued and trimmed off or folded to experiment with different edging techniques. Using two colors of material will bring out the patterns.

In twining, a sample can be made using eight to twelve warps and two colors of weft. By making a strap-like sample, you can try both methods of the half twist (see page 52). By using two colors and making twill patterns, you can practice both methods of the full twist (see page 53). The photo of the twining patterns is one such sample piece. The ends in the photo sample are done in wrapping and looping techniques (see page 61). The looping techniques are variations of the ones in the book to accommodate the uneven number of ends.

Project 1: Diagonal Checked Basket. This sample is made with cow and goat wallet leathers in black and tan. Color A—black, color B—tan.

1. Cut 12 lengths color A and 14 lengths color B 12" (30.5cm) long and ¼" (.64cm) wide.

2. Lay the 12 strips of color A vertically as warps on the working board.

3. Weave the strips of color B as wefts in check weave keeping the strips centered on the board.

4. Make a cardboard frame 4" (10.2cm) long by 2" (5.1cm) wide and 2" (5.1cm) high. Lay the frame on the woven center diagonally and fasten the corners of the center at the center points on the frame sides with a clothespin at each point.

5. Weave the corners, moving the clothespin over with each row woven.

6. Glue the edge warps and wefts at the 2" (5.1cm) edge line and let set.

7. Remove from the frame and trim the edges.

8. Cut two strips of black leather ¼" (.64cm) wide and 14" (35.6cm) long. Glue these strips on the edge of the basket inside and out. Skive, glue, and splice the ends.

9. Punch holes every ¼" (.64cm) in staggered pattern below and in the center of the edge strips.

10. Finish with the featherstitch braid using leather lacing to match either the black or the tan leather.

Project 1. Diagonal Checked Basket. Made with cow and goat wallet leathers in black and tan.

Project 2: Double Triangle or Starred Basket. Plastic clothesline is used for the warp and beige and green rug wool is used for the weft in this sample. Color A—beige, color B—green.

1. Cut 24 warps 13" (33.02cm) long. Work out the basket center as in Method 1 of the woven basket centers (see page 59), using color A.

2. After fastening the center pieces together, add an extra warp and weave in plain twine (see page 54) for 1" (2.54cm).

3. Take the back strand of color A and pin it to the closest warp with a clothespin so it will be carried along the warp (do not cut off). Needle in a strand of color B at the same point to take its place.

4. Weave in diagonal twill twine (see page 54) for 13 rows. Take the strand of color A from the warp where it is fastened and fasten up color B in its place.

5. Weave 11 rows of plain twine with color A.

6. Remove the strand of color B from the warp and pin up both strands of color A on two separate warps adjacent to each other, and needle in another strand of color B. Weave 5 rows of plain twine in color B.

7. Remove one strand of color A from the warp and replace it with one strand of color B. Weave in diagonal twill twine for four rows.

8. Remove the color B strand from the warp and replace it with the color A strand. Weave 3 rows of plain twine in color B.

9. Needle down one strand of color B for 1" (2.54cm) and cut off. Remove both strands of color A from the warps and replace one strand with the remaining color B strand. Weave for 5 rows in plain twine. Needle both color A ends down 1" (2.54cm) and cut off.

10. Trim warp ends to ¼" (.64cm). Edge the basket with the straight or wrapped edge (see page 61) in either method using the attached strand of color B to wrap the edge. Begin wrapping at the point where the color B strand is attached. Finish off.

Project 2. Double Triangle or Starred Basket. Plastic clothesline is used for the warp, and beige and green rug wool is used for the weft.

Paint Pot.   6" x 6½" x 6¼" diameter (15.24cm x 16.51cm x 15.87cm). This coiled piece is a study in form, color, and texture. The colors are shiny lime green, and textured shades of violet and blue-violet. The surface design was influenced by the shaping of the piece. It is coiled in figure-eight weave.

Simple Coiling Weaves

4

The rather vertical characteristics of plaiting and twining become modified in coiled basketry. The serpentine effect of the coiled spiral adds a multi-directional aspect to the baskets as well.

Before you learn the various weaves, you must learn how to start a coiled basket. There are two basic shapes in coiled basketry: round and oval. These shapes can be varied in many ways after you gain experience working with the basics.

STARTING A ROUND BASKET

Although there are many ways to start a round basket, each traditional basketweaver learned one particular way to begin. The contemporary weaver can make the choice of how to begin, and may even develop some individual or new techniques. It is good to know several ways to start because needs can change in contemporary basketry.

For now, however, choose one of the methods discussed here (the other ways can be mastered at a later time). First cut off several lengths of wrap material as explained in Chapter 2 so more material will not have to be measured off while working.

Method 1. Thread a tapestry needle with precut wrap. Wind the end of the wrap material around a pencil until the thickness is about half the diameter of the core material.

Step 1. Slip the circle off the pencil, keeping the wrap end tucked inside the circle.

Step 2. Now wrap the circle, using the needle to carry the material through the hole. Keep the wrap even and smooth, and be sure to cover the circle completely. Use a clothespin to keep the last wrap in place. Taper the end of a length of core material (see Chapter 2) so the taper will reach completely around the circle. Remove the clothespin and lay the tip of the core taper at the stopping point on the circle. A touch of glue will hold the core to the circle so it will not slip. Wrap the tapered core

Starting a Round Basket, Method 1, Step 1. Begin to wrap around the circle. Use a tapestry needle to carry the wrap through the hole.

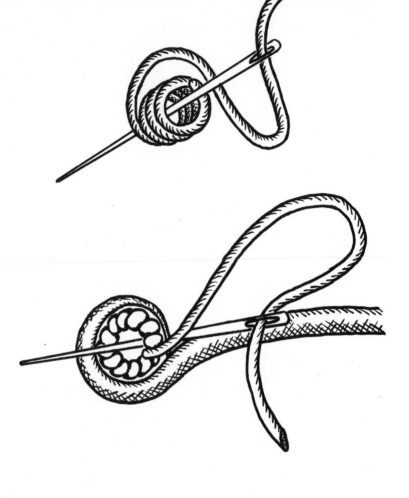

Step 2. Wrap a length of core with a tapered end around the circle as shown. Begin to wrap both the original circle and the taper cut.

on to the circle in the same way the original circle was wrapped. Now weaving can begin.

Method 2. Make a short taper on the end of a piece of core (see Chapter 2). Thread a tapestry needle with a precut length of wrap.

Step 1. Lay the wrap on top of the core with the end positioned about 1½" (3.81cm) beyond the taper cut.

Step 2. Hold the core and the wrap in the holding hand, and wrap away from the body with the working hand. The wrapping moves from the taper cut down the core toward the holding hand.

Step 3. Inching the holding hand ahead of the working hand, cover enough of the core to make a circle. The last wraps on the core should touch the unwrapped tip of the taper cut without making too big a hole in the center. Now hold the unwrapped tip and the core together and wrap over both, using the needle to take the wrap through the center.

Step 4. There should still be a little space in the center when the tip is covered because a hole will be needed when the weaving begins. If the hole seems too large on the first try, the start can be adjusted each time until the right size is found (the size of the wrap will also influence the size of the hole).

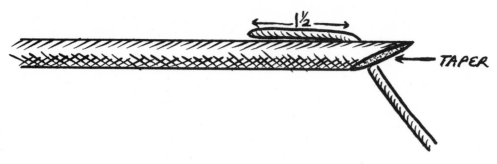

Starting a Round Basket, Method 2, Step 1. Overlap the ends of a piece of tapered core and a piece of wrap by about 1½" (3.81cm) as shown.

Step 2. Wrap the core at the taper cut, and move down toward the holding hand.

Step 3. Wrap enough of the core to make a circle. Needle the wrap through the center.

Step 4. Wrap over both the taper tip and the core until they are wrapped together.

Method 3. Tie several strands of wrap material together with a loose overhand knot so the knot is about half the thickness of the core material.

Step 1. One of the strands will become the precut piece of wrap and be threaded on the tapestry needle. The other strands can be of varying lengths. Hold all the short strands out of the way and wrap the knot with the long strand of wrap. Make a complete circle, going through the center of the knot for each wrap.

Step 2. Taper off the short ends and splice them together with a tapered core end. Now the center is complete for this method.

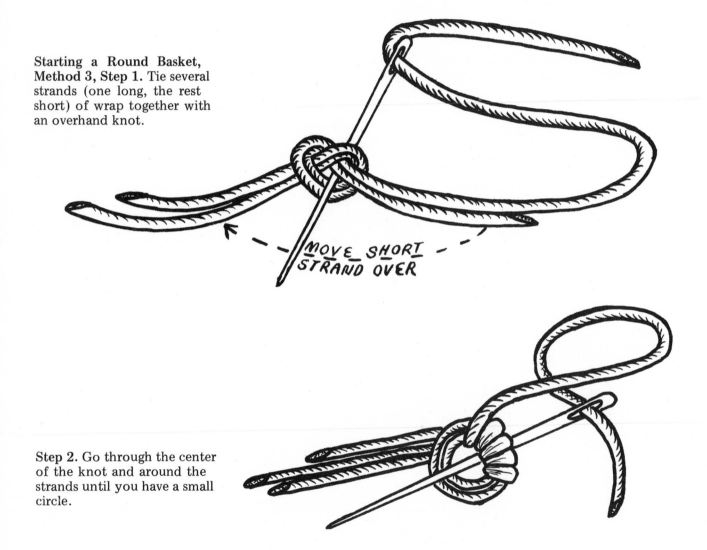

Starting a Round Basket, Method 3, Step 1. Tie several strands (one long, the rest short) of wrap together with an overhand knot.

MOVE SHORT STRAND OVER

Step 2. Go through the center of the knot and around the strands until you have a small circle.

Method 4. This is the most difficult of all the round starts because it needs to be handled more carefully. However, it is important to learn because there are times when it is the best way to begin.

Step 1. The core has a blunt end. Put a length of wrap on top of the core and begin wrapping at the end of the core.

Step 2. Moving toward the holding hand, wrap enough core so a little snail can be made. Push the end of the core past the last of the wrapping by at least ½" (1.27cm).

Step 3. Hold the circle tightly and needle through the center from the back of the work so the wrap is now going around two rows of core. Bring the wrap back up to the top of the core and the weaving can begin.

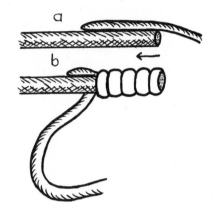

Starting a Round Basket, Method 4, Step 1. Overlap a length of blunt-ended core with a piece of wrap, and begin wrapping at the end of the core as shown.

Step 2. Wrap the core so a little snail can be made, and push the end of the core past the last wrap by about ½" (1.27cm).

Step 3. Needle through the center from the back and wrap around both rows of core.

STARTING AN OVAL BASKET

Use a piece of core with a blunt end, and fold it down about 1½" to 2" (3.8 to 5.1cm) (this short end should be kept on the working hand side all the time the initial weaving is done).

Step 1. Take uncut wrap directly from the ball, and place it on the core on the holding hand side so the end is 1½" (3.8cm) below the arch.

Step 2. Wrap around the core away from the holding hand until the top of the arch is covered (a hole will be formed below the arch if the wrapping is too long). Bring the wrap between the two pieces of core to the front of the work.

Step 3. Wrap around the holding hand side and bring it back between the pieces again. Wrap around the working hand side and bring it back between. Alternate sides in this way until the short side is covered to the end.

Step 4. Hold the remaining core in the holding hand, and wrap enough of the core so it can be curled around the end of the short piece and ½" (1.27cm) beyond (as in method 4 of the round baskets). Fasten in place with a clothespin. Now cut a working length of wrap from the ball, and thread it on to the tapestry needle. Remove the clothespin. Hold the core tightly against the previous work, and needle through from the back between the previous rows at the X point. Bring the wrap back up to the top of the core. Now the weave can begin.

Starting an Oval Basket, Step 1. Place the end of the wrap 1½" (3.8cm) below the core arch on the holding hand side as shown.

Step 2. Wrap the core covering only the arch.

Step 3. Wrap around each piece of the core alternately below the arch until the short end is covered.

Step 4. Wrap around the core moving toward the holding hand, until the wrapped core will reach the X when bent around the short wrapped end of the core. Needle through at the X using either the wrap or figure-eight weave.

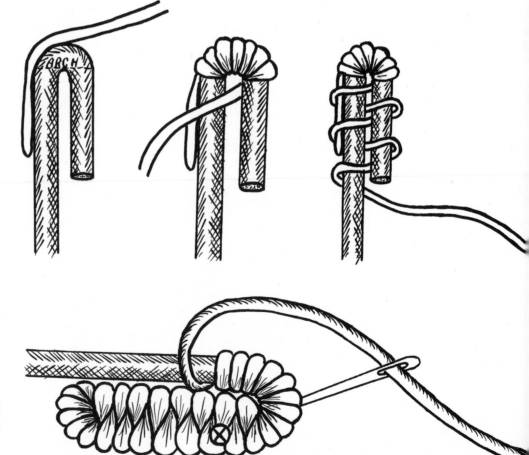

THE WRAP WEAVES

Although the basic weave of contemporary basketry is the figure-eight, the plain wrap weave is easier to learn because there is no reversal of weave.

Plain Wrap Weave. Hold the core, and wrap it three times, moving toward the holding hand.

Step 1. On the fourth wrap, needle through from the back and under the previous row. Bring the wrap back up and around the core so the long wrap fastens the two rows together.

Step 2. Wrap three times and needle through below the previous row from the back.

Step 3. The long wrap that fastens the core back on to the previous row creates a lovely random basketweave effect.

Plain Wrap Weave, Step 1. Wrap around the core three times working toward the holding hand. Needle through the center of the circle from the back of the work.

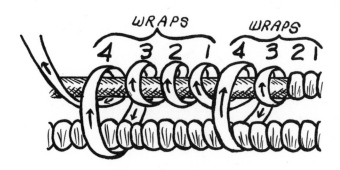

Step 2. Continue wrapping three times and needling through below the previous row from the back for this weave sequence.

Step 3. This weave produces a random pattern on the surface of the basket.

Patterned Wrap Weave. Start the patterned wrap weave in this manner.

Step 1. Follow the same instructions as in Step 1 of the plain wrap weave (see page 75).

Step 2. Follow Step 2 of the plain wrap weave in the same way to complete the first row.

Step 3. Position the long wraps in the succeeding rows so an even pattern results regardless of the number of wraps made on the core. In the illustration, the long wraps are placed to the left of the previous long wraps each time. They can be placed to the right or zigzagged back and forth for interesting patterns. The long wraps create a raised surface pattern.

The lines of long wraps begin to move apart as the size of the basket increases. Introduce new lines of long wraps or use figure-eights between the old lines of the pattern. Either will help to strengthen the basket wall.

Patterned Wrap Weave, Step 1. Follow Step 1 of the plain wrap weave.

Step 2. Follow Step 2 of the plain wrap weave.

Step 3. Position the long wraps in each row so the result is a definite pattern.

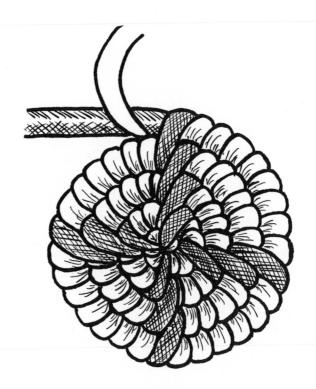

Traditional Wrap Weave. The traditional wrap weave differs from the plain wrap weave in several respects. It consists of a continuous series of long wraps over two rows. The core is not wrapped between long wraps. Following the illustration, wrap toward the body. Needle between each wrap of the previous row from the front. A space will remain on the core between each wrap.

It is best to use firm wraps such as rug yarns, raffia, flat reed, plastic tubing or strips, but softer yarns can be used with a little more effort. The traditional wrap weave has a smooth, even look, and it is a much stronger weave than the plain wrap weave.

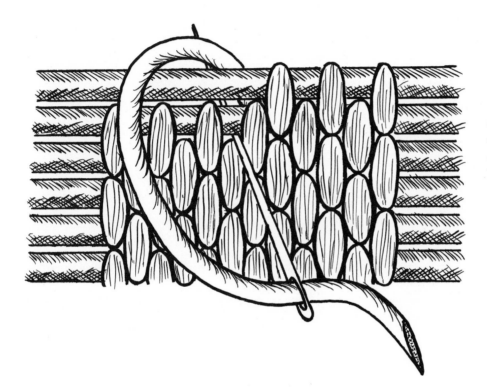

Traditional Wrap Weave. Fasten both rows together on each wrap by needling below the lower row from the front. A small space remains between each wrap until the next row is worked.

VARIATIONS ON THE WRAP WEAVE

Four more variations can be developed from the plain wrap weave: pebble, knot, lace, and wigwam weaves.

Pebble Weave. Make the plain wrap weave sequence, but before beginning to wrap up and around the core in the next sequence, needle around the long wrap or post. Make sure to encircle both the back and front strands of the post with the wrap. Pull through and bring the wrap around to the front again between the core and the previous row. Continue the plain wrap sequence, wrapping the post in the same way. Do not spread the rows apart while doing this weave. The result will be a pebbly surface texture.

Knot Weave. Follow directions for the pebble weave, but hold the two rows slightly apart while the fastening is made. This will give an open look.

Lace Weave. Follow directions for the knot weave, but wrap the post twice for a lacy result. These weaves work better with heavier materials,

Pebble Weave. After making the wrap weave sequence, needle around the post enclosing both front and back long wraps and pull through. Bring the wrap between the two rows to the front again before wrapping the core in the next weave sequence.

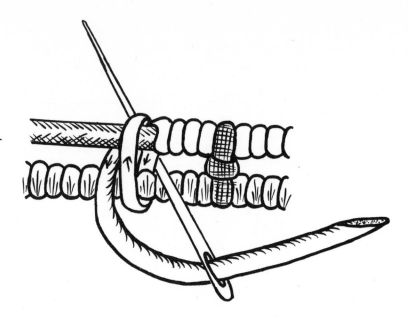

Wigwam Weave, Step 1. Place one wrap slightly to the right and one to the left in making this variation of the wrap weave.

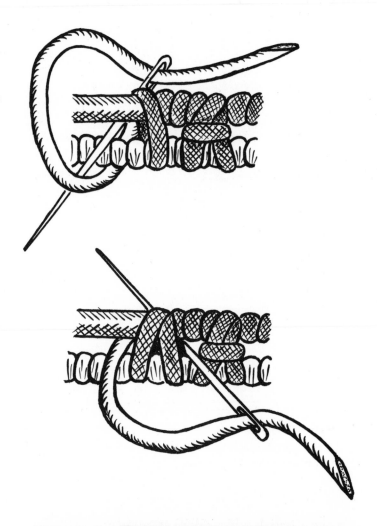

Step 2. Needle around both posts as shown.

Step 3. This variation of the wigwam weave has three posts: left, center, and right. Needle the wrap around all three posts as shown.

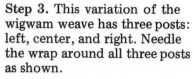

but if you want to use lightweight wraps, then wrap several times for a heavier post, and wrap around the post several times for strength.

Wigwam Weave. You can make a particularly beautiful decorative pattern with a variation of the pebble weave. Named by one of my students, the wigwam weave should be done with two colors to be really effective.

Step 1. Follow directions in Chapter 2 for adding new wrap, and add a new color. Fasten the long wrap to the previous row, but do not place the needle straight down from the top. Place the needle slightly to the working hand side.

Step 2. Pull wrap through, bring it up and over the core. Needle through under the previous row slightly to the holding hand side and bring back up and around the core. Needle around both posts as in the pebble weave, and continue with the next sequence.

Step 3. This weave can be done with three posts as well. Needle the wrap right, center, and left, and then wrap the posts together in the same way. When either of these variations is done correctly, the weave looks like little rows of wigwams.

FIGURE-EIGHT WEAVES

There is a good reason that the figure-eight weave is the basic weave of contemporary coiled basketry. It has a smooth, even look that combines with all the other decorative weaves easily. It is strong because the core is held tightly in place with a reverse weave.

In method 4 of the round basket starts (see page 73), one change must be made before the figure-eight weave can be done. After Step 2, hold the circle tightly and bring the wrap between the wrapped and unwrapped core to the front of the work. Needle through the center from the front and pull through very carefully. Bring the wrap forward between the rows again. Now you are ready to do the figure-eight weaves.

Basic Figure-Eight Weave. Wrap the core three times in the same way as the wrap weave, and bring the wrap between the core and the previous row to the front of the work.

Step 1. With the needle, pass under the previous row from the front and pull through.

Step 2. Bring the wrap forward between the rows before wrapping the core again.

Some people like to wrap long sections of core without fastening back with the figure-eight weave. This is especially true when colors are involved in the design. These long unfastened areas can give a very interesting look to the piece, but they weaken the work. If the piece were to be used as a workbasket, it would soon lose its strength. If used as a sculptural piece, the basket must be stuffed or supported from the inside. It is preferable to build the sculptural effects into the piece so it will withstand time and use. A better solution for a clean color line is the pierced figure-eight weave.

Although the usual number of wraps on the core is three, you can occasionally extend the wraps to as many as six without problems if the work is really tight. If the work seems to need extra strength, reduce the

Basic Figure-Eight Weave, Step 1. Wrap the core three times. Bring the wrap between the two rows to the front and needle through below the previous row.

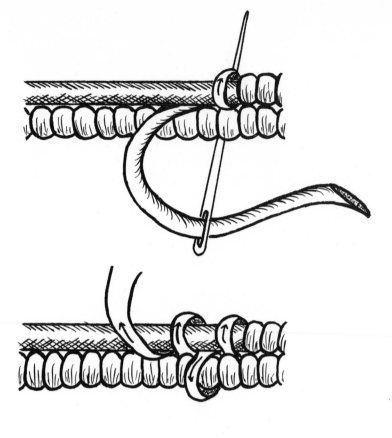

Step 2. Bring the wrap between the rows to the front before wrapping again.

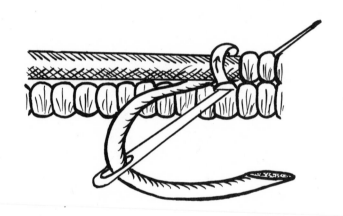

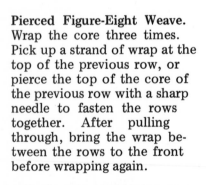

Pierced Figure-Eight Weave. Wrap the core three times. Pick up a strand of wrap at the top of the previous row, or pierce the top of the core of the previous row with a sharp needle to fasten the rows together. After pulling through, bring the wrap between the rows to the front before wrapping again.

number of wraps to two, or eliminate them entirely, thus using the figure-eight continuously. Use this extra strength at points of stress as on the lift point row (see page 82) or at the base of narrow neck curves in large, heavy pieces. In workbaskets, the edge must be strengthened.

Pierced Figure-Eight Weave. If a new color is being added, the pierced figure eight is used so the new color does not cross over the previous row. Thread the wrap onto a sharp tapestry needle. Wrap the core three times, and bring the wrap between the core and the previous row. Use the point of the needle either to pick up a strand of wrap on top of the previous row or to pierce the top of the core ever so slightly. Pull the wrap through to the back, and then bring it forward between the rows to the front of the work as in the regular figure-eight before wrapping the core again. This will leave a clean color line between the rows.

Plaque using Figure-Eight and Wrap Weaves. The figure-eight weave has a smooth, even look that combines with all the other decorative weaves easily.

Adding New Wrap Material, Figure-Eight Weaves. Wrap the core three times, and lay the end of the old wrap on top of the core. Cut off any excess leaving 1" to 1½" (2.54cm to 3.8cm). Lay the new wrap parallel to the old wrap. Wrap around the core from the back and between the rows to the front. Then needle through below the previous row, pull through and bring the wrap back between the rows to the front before wrapping the core.

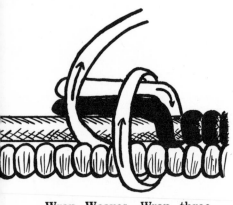

Wrap Weaves. Wrap three times, and lay the end of the old wrap on top of the core. Cut off any excess leaving 1" to 1½" (2.54cm to 3.8cm). Lay the new wrap parallel to the old wrap. Carry the wrap down the back, and needle through under the previous row from the back. Wrap up over both rows, and then bring the wrap down and under the core before wrapping again.

ADDING NEW WRAP MATERIAL

A good place to add new wrap is after wrapping the core. There should be 1" to 1½" (2.54 to 3.8cm) remaining at this point. Place the end of the old wrap on top of the core and fasten with a clothespin so it will not slip while threading the new wrap on the needle. Remove the pin. On top of the core, place the end of the new piece of wrap on top of or beside the end of the old wrap.

If you are working in the figure-eight weave, bring the wrap down, around, and forward between the rows. Needle through below the previous row in front of the work. Pull through, and bring the wrap up and between the two rows again. Now the new wrap is fastened well. Continue weaving in the usual manner.

If you are working in the wrap weave, bring the wrap down and needle below the previous row from the back. Pull through and bring the wrap up and over the top of the core. Now bring the wrap between the rows again before starting to wrap the core for the next wrap sequence.

When needling through the first time, pull slowly and carefully. A big yank will sometimes pull the wrap loose and it must be started over again. When covering the wrap ends, keep them on top of the core and in sight so the little ends are always tucked in and are fastened down under the wrap.

THE CENTER POINT AND LIFT POINT LINES

Now some points about making the basket. The first thing you need to do is find a point of reference, whether working flat or sculpturally. The beginning point of the basket is the end of the core. From that point an imaginary line can be drawn all the way to the edge of the piece (see center point line illustration). This is the center point line—everything (each row of design, regular color rows), starts and ends at this line. This is where the basket begins to lift up from the base (see the illustration of lift point).

As the wall of the basket begins to rise, the lift point line (an imaginary line drawn from the lift point at the base of the basket) takes over as the point of reference from the center point line. The side of the basket with the lift point line has a definite tilt, while the other side appears more even. The basket should be finished off at the lift point line.

The lift point is quite drastic in a cylindrical basket. It moves directly on top of the last row which creates the floor of the basket immediately. A rounder shape allows the lift point to move up more slowly.

Achieving the Lift Point. Hold the core above the previous row while fastening the wrap. Some people have trouble making the lift hold its position the first few times it is fastened. This is especially true for a very slight lift. Take the core in the holding hand and the basket in the working hand and give a slight yank. If a lift does not automatically appear, the work is firmer than that of most beginners and you must pull harder.

SHAPING A BASKET

Shaping is simple. All you need to do is place the core in the direction that the basket will go, then fasten the wrap to the previous row. Put the core on top of the flat base for a cylindrical basket. To decrease the

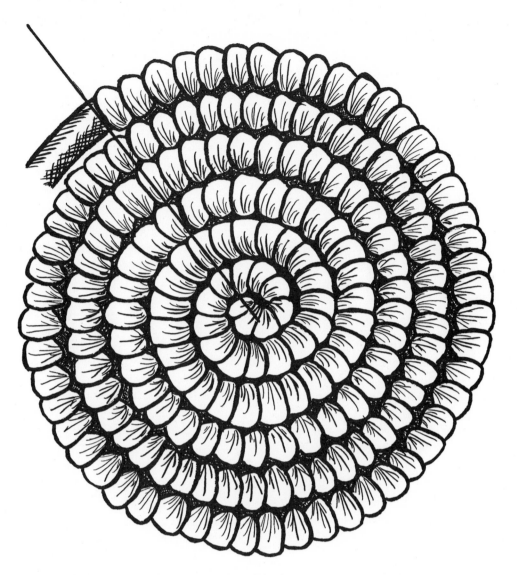

Center Point Line. The beginning of the basket coil is the starting point for the center point line. Begin the lift point on this line.

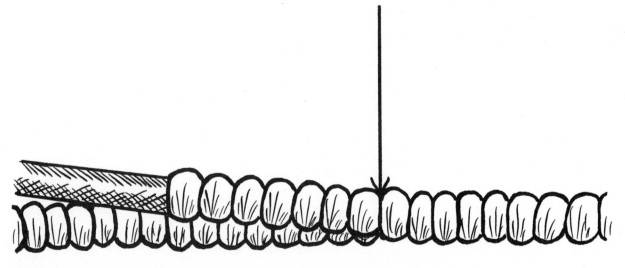

Lift Point Line. The point of reference on the side of the basket is the lift point line. Rows of designs and colors begin and end here. The basket is finished off at this line.

basket size or to move inward, place the core toward the inside of the previous row. The outward placement of the core will enlarge the basket size or form a lip at the top.

Some basket shapes are more beautiful than others. Baskets with round or curved sides are more graceful but not always the easiest to achieve. The slower the lift, the more oblate the curve. The faster the rise, the more conical or cylindrical.

Cylindrical shapes are the easiest to make, but they present a problem. The steepness of the lift point is accentuated on that side of the basket. All of the rows have a slanted appearance, giving the lift point side the look of the Leaning Tower of Pisa.

Solutions for the Cylindrical Basket. One way to help the problem is to make designs on the side opposite the lift point to direct attention away from the problem area. You can also break the line by changing directions on the basket (see the illustrations).

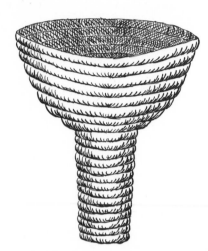

Solutions for Cylindrical Baskets. 1. The straight sides of the basket can flare out into a spherical shape at the top.

2. The straight sides turn at right angles to move outward before turning upward at right angles again. A looped edge softens the look of the cylindrical basket.

STRENGTHENING THE BASKET WALLS

Wrap the core as tightly as possible. Pull tightly on the wrap after fastening to the previous row. If the basket seems soft no matter what is done, pull *gently* on the core with the holding hand every few wraps in the same way the lift point was achieved. This helps to strengthen the basket by tightening the wrap on to the core. As more baskets are made, the muscles of the hands, wrists, and arms will become stronger, and better controlled baskets will be the result.

Since most people have to build up their knowledge and strength, their work varies a good deal in the beginning. It is best to plan small projects first, and the improvement will be seen from basket to basket. Sometimes students will be overcome with enthusiasm and want to take on a large project right at the start. As the basket progresses, the work becomes firmer, stronger, and tighter, and the piece becomes misshapen. If a large project must be done, choose a strong core material such as those mentioned in Chapter 2. The structural strength of the material cannot be affected as much by the weaver's change in ability. Also, choose a strong wrap material that is not elastic. Work as tightly and firmly as possible.

Traditionally, basketweavers have worked on the outside of baskets as one would work on the outside of ceramic pots. There are good reasons for this. First, there is better control of the shaping. Second, as the basket makes an abrupt turn toward the center, or the basket opening becomes quite small, it is easier to work from the outside. Third, the weaves tend to look better on the outside of the work. Reasons for breaking this rule will be discussed in Chapter 7.

Although the work looks better on one side, great care should be taken to make both inside and outside look neat and attractive when doing an open basket that will be viewed from both sides.

FINISHING OFF THE BASKET

In traditional basketry, the basket is often finished with the core stopping abruptly along the edge. However, in contemporary basketry, this type of ending looks rather unfinished. The general consensus is that the edge should be as smooth and straight as possible.

Since coiled basketry is formed as a spiral, the edge has a tilted look as

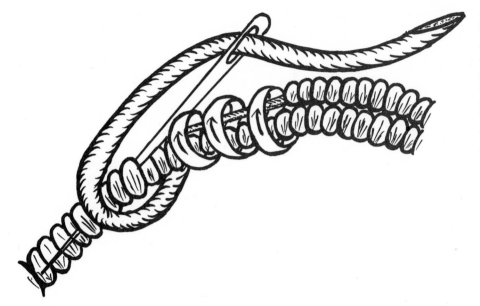

Finishing Off the Basket.
Taper the end of the core at the lift point line. Work up to the edge of the taper. Wrap the taper and the previous row together until this wrapping has passed the tip of the core by ½" (1.27cm). Needle under the wrap, pull through, and cut off to fasten the wrap end.

it moves up. When you reach the last row, work around the top until within 2" to 3" (5.1 to 7.62cm) of the lift point line. Lay the core along the top, and cut off the end of the core slightly beyond the lift point line. Taper the end of the core with a long gradual taper. If the piece is flat like a trivet, use the center point line instead of the lift point line.

Be sure the working wrap is long enough to cover the taper plus about 3" (7.62cm) more. If the wrap is beginning to get too short, cut it off before the taper begins and add a new piece. It is better to cut it off at this point, where it is easy to add on, than to run out at a very awkward point.

Wrap the last of the core until it becomes difficult to work (see the illustration). If worked too close to the end, the tip of the core may come loose, and the end can look very thin and spindly. Wrap the tip of the core end and the previous row together. Continue needling around the top row for about ½" (1.27cm) or more past the tip. If the core is large, wrap ¾" (2cm) or more. Needle under the wrap for about an inch (2.54cm), pull through, and cut off the remaining wrap (see illustration). If it is difficult to work the needle under the wrap because the wrapping is good and tight, use a smaller diameter needle.

Making a Lid. The shaping of the lid should accent and enhance the basket. It is easy to design a lid for the cylindrical basket, but the spherical shape can be a little more challenging. The top can fit into the basket like the top of a jack-o-lantern, fit over the edge like a cap, or lift up at the edge in a reverse curve. A lid must have a central point of interest, whether it be a handle or a decorative object. This point of interest can be functional or not.

In making the lid, the process is the same as making a basket with the exception of the start. If the handle or decorative object is to be closed like a basket start, begin there first. The lid then becomes an extension of this object.

If the decorative object is to be a sculptural experience on the basket lid incorporating surface coiling, leave an unwrapped extension at the center to be completed later (see Chapter 7 for ideas).

The lid can be formed to fit the basket opening, or a base extension can be formed after it is finished.

SAMPLE PROJECTS

A good project is a flat plaque using all of the different weaves. Use each weave for three to five rows. It will give practice in making each weave, and it will be a good reference when you wish to use a particular weave or technique later. The piece can be made gradually as new weaves are introduced in the book. In making a plaque, you can focus on the construction of the weaves without having to concentrate on shaping, too.

Project 1. Looped Edge Basket. This sample basket is made with #120 ⅜" (9.5mm) jute for the core. Any type of rope will do. The wrap is heavy yellow and orange rug wool. Color A—orange, color B—yellow.

1. Using any type circle start, work three rows of figure-eight in color A.

2. Cut off color A, and add color B. Make one row with the following variation of the plain wrap weave: wrap three times, needle back to the previous row twice, making two long wraps parallel to each other. Repeat this variation to the end of the row.

3. Using color B, make two rows of figure-eight weave.

4. Cut off color B, and add color A. Make one row of the wrap weave variation in Step 2.

5. Using color A, weave two rows in figure-eight, beginning the slight lift for a curved base in the first row. Cut off color A.

6. Adding color B, make a row of knot weave with two parallel posts.

7. Using color B, make one row of figure-eight weave. Cut off color B.

8. Add color A. Follow the directions in Step 6.

9. This edging example has six loops around the edge. More or less may be desired according to the size of the core and wrap. Divide the distance into equal spaces. Mark them with yarn, if necessary. These will be the fastening points for the loops.

10. Using color A, wrap enough of the core to make a shallow V from the edge that will reach the first fastening spot. Fasten down with three continuous figure-eights. Continue around the edge in the same manner to the last loop. Cut off the core so the taper will lie on the beginning of the rise of the first loop.

11. Work to the taper, and finish off.

Project 1. Looped Edge Basket. Made with jute for the core, but any type of rope will do. The wrap is heavy yellow and orange rug wool.

Project 2. Spiral Basket. This sample basket is made with #72 ½" (1.27cm) jute for the core, but any type of rope will do. The wrap is a shiny acrylic yarn (single ply) with a smooth finish. Color A—deep gold, color B—brown.

1. Using any circle start, weave in the basic figure-eight weave with color A, until the base measures about 3" (7.62cm) in diameter.

2. Planning for an angle about 50° from the base, begin to raise the sides in a gradual curving slope. Work three rows in this manner.

3. Cut off color A. Add color B, and do three sequences of the three post wigwam weave. Cut off color B.

4. Add color A, and continue the row in basic figure-eight weave, until you reach color B. Cut off color A.

5. Add color B. Work across the color B area with basic figure-eight weave, making sure the fastenings fall between the wigwam knots. Now add three more wigwam weave sequences. Cut off color B.

6. Add color A. Work in basic figure-eight weave until you reach the edge of the color B area. Now work in the pierced figure-eight weave across the top of the block above the first three wigwam sequences (this block is the first step of the spiral that will curl up the side of the basket). Cut off color A.

7. Add color B. Work across the color B area with the basic figure-eight weave, adjusting the fastenings as in Step 5. Add three more wigwam sequences. Cut off color B.

8. Add color A. Work in basic figure-eight weave until you reach the edge of the next color B block. Now work in pierced figure-eight weave across the top of the block (three wigwam sequences). Cut off color A.

9. Repeat Steps 7 and 8 until all the blocks or steps have been completed.

10. Add color B and work across the next block and add three more wigwam sequences. Cut off color B.

11. Add color A. Work around the row in the basic figure-eight weave to the lift point line. At this point you will begin to decrease the size of the basket by placing the core inward so the angle will be about 60°. This is a flatter angle, and the basket will decrease in size more rapidly. Continue working in the figure-eight weave to the edge of the next color B block. Change to the pierced figure-eight weave to the end of the block as before. Cut off color A.

12. Repeat Steps 7 and 8 as you continue to decrease the size of the basket until the 13th block has been completed. Cut off color A.

13. Add color B. Work across the solid color B area with basic figure-eight weave, making adjustments for the wigwam knots. Now make continuous wigwams around the row until the edge of the 14th block is reached.

14. Using color B, weave two rows in basic figure-eight, and finish off.

Project 2. Spiral Basket. Made with jute for the core, but any type of rope will do. The wrap is shiny acrylic yarn (single ply) with a smooth finish. Colors are deep gold and brown.

Leather Imbricated Basket. 3¾'' x 8¼'' x 5½'' diameter (9.52cm x 26.67cm x 13.97cm). This coiled basket was woven by Carol Large of Huntington Beach, California, in wools ranging from yellow to rust over braided clothesline. Dark brown leather was looped before it was imbricated in the beading weave.

Decorative Techniques for Coiling and Plaiting

5

Exciting textural effects can be introduced into coiled basketry by using decorative techniques and weaves. Although these techniques have a complex look, they are not necessarily more complicated to do. Some of these techniques can be used as a basis for adding further decorative elements.

THE RIPPLE WEAVE

The ripple weave creates a textural effect by using two cores of different diameters. The difference in the core sizes gives the basket surface a wavy or rippled look. The basket may be made entirely in this technique, or the weave may be added for interest in an otherwise plain surface.

There are two ways to achieve the ripple weave. In the first method, which is the more traditional, the different sized cores are added at the same time. In the second method the rows are added one at a time. The second method is easier, but the core sizes have a tendency to be more concealed in the work. The greater the difference in the core sizes, the more definite the rippled look.

Since the basket pattern depends on double rows, the best shaping for an entire basket of ripple weave is a spherical shape. The lift transition of the double row is too wide to lift drastically (as in the typical cylindrical basket) without giving the piece a misshapen look. The edge must be rounded before moving up into the straight sides.

The core material should be smooth with no fibers. The technique is much like twining, and the beating and sliding of the wrap material over the core will raise the fibers to the basket surface. Material like jute can cause problems, but smooth clothesline rope would be excellent. Check Chapter 1 for other materials to use.

Starting the Ripple Weave Basket. Choose two different sizes of core material. Taper the ends of both pieces of core, then place them together, with the larger piece on top. Thread your needle with a piece of wrap material. Treating both cores as a single piece, make a circle start using

Method 2 (see page 70). Keep the larger piece of core on the outside of the circle. Measure several yards of each core and cut off with a taper (this will aid in splicing, if necessary).

For simplification, the larger core will be core 1 and the smaller core will be core 2. Following directions in Chapter 1, make butterflies with the core pieces. This keeps the cores short and up out of the way so the work can be done by weaving in and out with the wrap. Otherwise, a needle has to be used for each intersection with the core and makes the work slow and tedious.

Method 1. Hold the two cores together as described above. Then bring the wrap up and over the top of core 1.

Step 1. Make a figure-eight, fastening cores 1 and 2 together. Tighten the wrap carefully at each intersection by pulling the wrap against the covered area. When tightening the ripple weave, hold on to both pieces of core firmly. The small core has a tendency to buckle unless held tightly.

Step 2. Now take the wrap over core 1, between cores 1 and 2 to the front, and then between core 2 and the previous row to the back. Tighten each intersection. Needle below the previous row and pull through to the front. Weave the wrap over the previous row, under core 2, and over core 1 up to the top again. Tighten the intersections. This completes the entire ripple weave sequence.

Repeat the two parts of the entire sequence for the ripple weave. Check to be sure the wrap is covering the core back and front. If not, beat back against the work with a needle or your fingernails.

As the basket increases in size, adjust the ripple weave sequence to keep the weaving in a straight line and to be sure that all of the areas are covered. It may be necessary to use two continuous figure-eights over cores 1 and 2 between the ripple weave fastening, and occasionally an extra wrap may need to be made on core 1. It will be obvious to the eye when these adjustments need to be made. After the basket stops increasing in size, drop all of the extra wraps and figure-eights, if necessary, to keep the work uniform. This is the stronger of the two ripple weave methods.

Method 2. Bring the wrap forward between core 2 and the previous row. Work around the row using the basic figure-eight weave to attach core 2 to the circle. When you reach the unwrapped edge of core 1, make a butterfly of the core 2 wrap, leaving the needle threaded on the wrap. This will keep the length of wrap out of the way while working on core 1.

Take a new length of wrap and thread this on another needle. Needle under the wrapped section of core 1 about 1" (2.54cm) back from the unwrapped edge of the core. Pull through until the end disappears under the wrap. Now work around core 1 using the basic figure-eight weave to fasten core 1 to core 2. When you reach the end of this row, make this wrap, including the needle, into a butterfly, and work with core 2 as before. Continue alternating this way throughout the basket.

This method tends to be slower and more cumbersome, and it is not as strong as the other method, but it covers the core more easily. Choose the method that seems better for you.

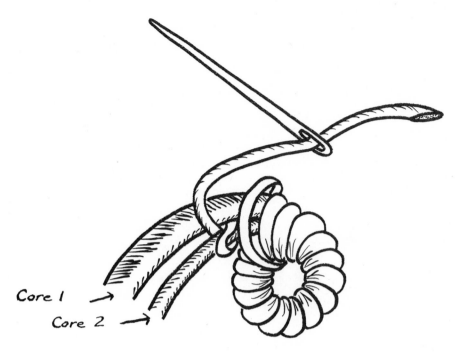

Core 1

Core 2

Ripple Weave, Method 1, Step 1. Use cores of different diameters, keeping the larger core on the outside as shown. Make a figure-eight, fastening cores 1 and 2 together. Tighten the wrap at each intersection.

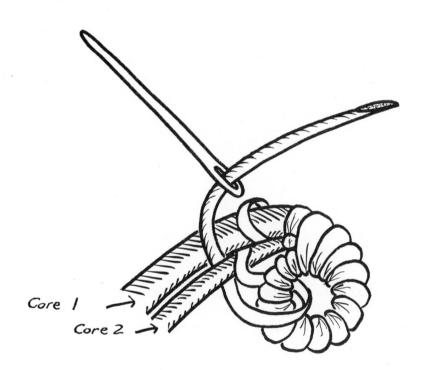

Core 1

Core 2

Step 2. Weave the wrap over and in back of core 1, between and down in front of core 2, then between and in back of the previous row. Needle through under the previous row and pull the wrap through. Weave in back of core 2 and to the front of core 1.

The Ripple Weave, Comparison of Methods 1 and 2. The ripple weave creates a textural effect by using two cores of different diameters.

Finishing Off the Ripple Weave Basket. Do not carry the smaller core through to the end of the basket. Finishing off using only the larger core gives a stronger edge and a smoother look. The basket should have an extra row of the larger core at the top edge.

Method 1. Work to within 2" (5.08cm) of the lift point line where core 2 is to be cut off. Place core 2 on the previous row to the lift point line, then cut off the core slightly beyond that point and taper the end. Work to the beginning of the taper cut. Following the illustration, do continuous ripple weave fastenings to about ¼" (6.35mm) from the tip of the taper, holding the taper and core carefully. This work must be done by needling through each intersection while holding the taper between the fingers so it cannot bend or come loose. Now hold the taper against core 1 and work in continuous figure-eights over the tip and beyond until the row begins to flatten out on to the previous row. Work one more row of core 1 and finish off.

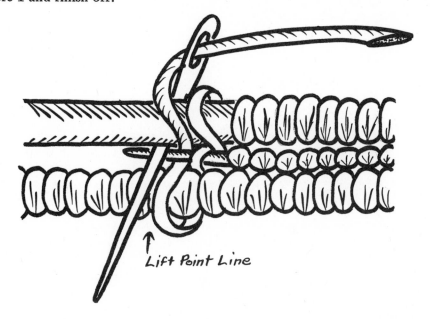

Lift Point Line

Finishing Off the Ripple Weave, Method 1. Cut core 2 off beyond the lift point line, and taper the core. Hold the 2 cores and the previous row and weave continuous ripple weave fastenings to within ¼" (.64cm) of the tip of the taper cut. Hold the tip next to core 1. Do continuous figure-eight fastenings until the row begins to level out.

Method 2. Work the basket up to the last row of core 2. Cut off the core slightly past the lift point line as in method 1 and taper the end. Finish the row up to the beginning of the taper cut. Cut off the wrap for core 2 leaving about 1" to 1½" (2.54 to 3.81cm) and place this alongside the tapered end of the core. Pick up core 1 and work the row up to this point. Hold the wrap end, the tapered core, and core 1 together as a unit and work the figure-eight weave to within ¼" (6.35mm) of the taper tip. Now do continuous figure-eights until the core has lots its angled look and is flattened out against the previous row. Work one more row and finish off.

The Ripple Weave as an Accent. Use a smaller core than the basic core size when adding ripple weave accents. The addition of a smaller core will be less obvious in the continuing spiral of the basket.

Adding the Second Core. Taper the end of the smaller core. Make several continuous figure-eights prior to the lift point line to open up the space a bit between the core and the previous row. Following the illustration, place the tapered end of core 2 below core 1 at the lift point line, and continue working in continuous figure-eights until the ripple weave can

Adding the Second Core for the Ripple Weave as an Accent. Taper the end of a smaller piece of core. Place the tip of this core at the lift point line between the core and the previous row. Hold the cores together and work in continuous figure-eights until the two cores can be pulled apart and woven separately without pulling the smaller core out.

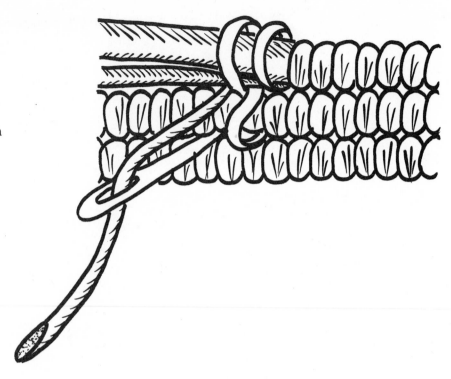

be worked without pulling core 2 loose when separating from core 1. If carefully worked, the chosen ripple weave can begin before the tapered end is covered. This helps to make the transition look more even and gradual. Work until you are ready to discontinue core 2. Finish off core 2 using the method described earlier.

THE BLANKET WEAVE

The blanket weave is similar to the blanket or buttonhole stitch in sewing or embroidery. It makes an interesting edging for an opening or along the lip of a basket. It makes an excellent ridge for attaching decorative material or fringes (see Chapter 6).

Making the Blanket Weave. Make a figure-eight fastening, and lay the wrap on the front of the core as if making another wrap.

Step 1. Place the holding hand thumb against the core and hook the wrap around the thumb toward the front. Needle through under the previous row from the front and pull through until the loop is almost tight. Slip the needle through the loop on the thumb from the back.

Step 2. Slip out the thumb and pull the wrap tight. Make a figure-eight fastening and wrap the core once. This is the blanket weave fastening sequence.

Repeat the blanket weave sequence across the opening or around the top of the piece as often as desired. The number of wraps between the knots can vary as long as they are the same distance apart or make a pattern. There should be a space of at least three wraps between the knots, or they will not show up very well. Use figure-eight fastenings between for strength if the spaces between the knots are more than three wraps. Use the blanket weave over the previously wrapped row around the edge of the basket to keep the look even.

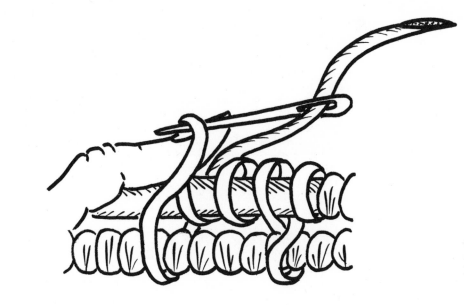

Blanket Weave, Step 1. Bring up the wrap and hook over the thumb as shown. Needle under the previous row, and pull through. Bring the wrap up and needle through the thumb loop from the back.

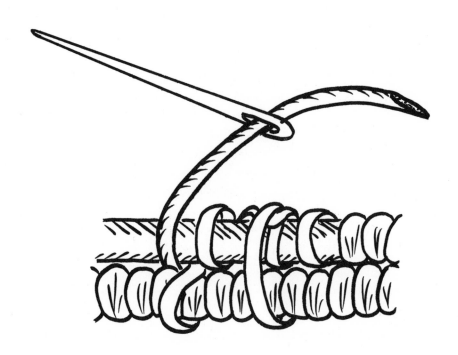

Step 2. Pull the thumb loop tight. Make a figure-eight fastening, and wrap the core one time.

The Open Cycloids, Step 1.
Make three continuous figure-
eights at the shaded area. Wrap
enough core to make a coil.

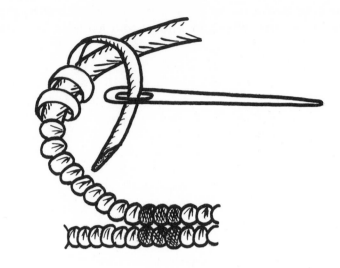

Step 2. Shape the coil and
place in back of and a little
ahead of the ascending leg
as shown. Fasten down with
three continuous figure-eights.

Step 3. Wrap the core for a
second coil and place it in
back of and overlapped by the
first coil as shown. Fasten in
place with three continuous
figure-eights.

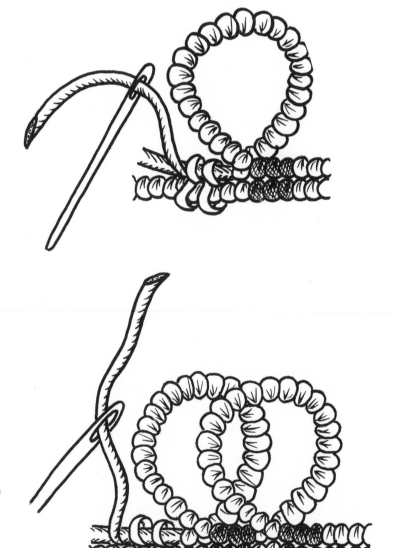

Keep the knot positioned at the top of the core for an edging decoration. The wrap material should be smooth and hard-surfaced. Handspuns and fuzzy materials cover up the little ridge knots and make them unrecognizable. See Chapter 1 for types of materials to use.

Place the knots on the basket surface if the blanket weave is being used for attachments. Place the knots as close together as needed. You do not have to be concerned about patterning because the ridges will be covered with the attachments. The knots can be placed anywhere. The blanket weave can be used to attach all types of decorative elements such as beads, shells, feathers, as well as fringe, embroidery, and surface weaving. The best place to add new wrap in the blanket weave is after making the knot.

THE CYCLOIDS

The three cycloid weaves are both decorative and functional. Except for the intertwined cycloid, they are not weaves in the true sense, but they can be used in the body of the basket for an interesting effect.

The cycloids can be used as decorative rows or as beautiful edgings. All three methods can be used within the same basket, but not in the same row or you will twist the basket out of shape.

Make three continuous figure-eights prior to the lift point line before starting any of the cycloids. This gives strength to the ascending leg of the coil. In the cycloid illustrations, continuous figure-eights are shown as shaded areas.

The Open Cycloids. First make three continuous figure-eights.

Step 1. Wrap the core until there is enough length to curl the piece around in a single coil that has a round and comfortable shape without being cramped or sprawled.

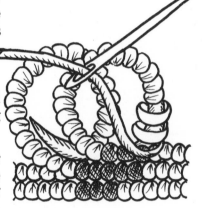

Step 2. Be sure to wrap the core tightly. Push the wraps close together or spaces will appear between the wraps when the core is bent. Place the descending leg of the coil behind the ascending leg and a little ahead of the takeoff point. Fasten the coil to the previous row with three continuous figure-eights.

Step 3. Wrap the core again to make another coil. Place this coil behind the first so the first coil partially overlaps it. Check to see that the size and shape is the same as the first, then fasten down in the same way. Repeat this sequence the desired number of times. Slightly decrease the height of the cycloids so the height of the last coil will be as high as the beginning coil. This gives a more even look to the edge or the row.

Finishing Off the Open Cycloid Row. Place the last coil between the adjacent coils, making sure they overlap it equally. Taper the core at the end so it lies on top of the takeoff point of the first coil (see the illustration). Wrap the tapered core on to the ascending leg at the takeoff point in the usual way to finish a basket.

The Closed Cycloids. Make three continuous figure-eights.

Step 1. Wrap enough core to make the first coil. Place it in the same way as the first open cycloid coil. Before starting the second coil, shape the unwrapped core in a coil so the sides of the coils touch. These coils do

Finishing Off the Open Cycloid Row. Place the last coil between the previous coil and the first coil. Taper the end of the core allowing the tip to lie on the ascending leg of the first coil as shown. Fasten the core in place with three continuous figure eights, and wrap the tapered tip of the core to the ascending leg of the first coil. Needle under the wrap, pull through and cut off.

99

The Closed Cycloids, Step 1. Complete the first coil, place on the previous row and fasten down as shown. Place the unwrapped core on the previous row and make a coil to check shape and size. Make continuous figure-eights to the point the ascending leg leaves the previous row.

Step 2. Wrap enough core to reach the place where the coil touches the side of the first coil. Make three continuous figure-eights at this point. Wrap the rest of the coil and fasten onto the previous row with three continuous figure-eights.

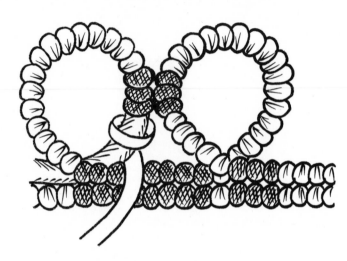

not overlap. Gauge the distance needed on the previous row to reach the takeoff point of the second coil. Work in continuous figure-eights to that point.

Step 2. Wrap enough of the core to take it around to the point on the side of the first coil where the coils are to be fastened together. Make three continuous figure-eights at this point. Continue wrapping the core until you reach the fastening point on the descending leg of the coil. Fasten with three continuous figure-eights. Repeat this sequence throughout the row. Finish off the row in the same manner as the open cycloids.

The Intertwined Cycloids. This technique looks more complicated than it is. Determine both the length of the piece required to make each coil and the space the coil will fill in the row. Then measure the circumference of the basket to find out how many coils will be needed. Measure this length on the core plus one circumference length and cut off. The core, needle, and wrap must be threaded through the previous row each time before fastening the new coil to the row.

Make the first coil and fasten down as with the open cycloids. After wrapping the length for the next coil, thread the end of the core and the needle through the previous coil opening from the front. As this is done, hold on to the piece where the wrapping stopped so it will not slip. This must be held by hand because a clothespin will not slip through the coil.

After pulling through, always check the size and shape of each new coil before fastening down. It is harder to determine the length of the

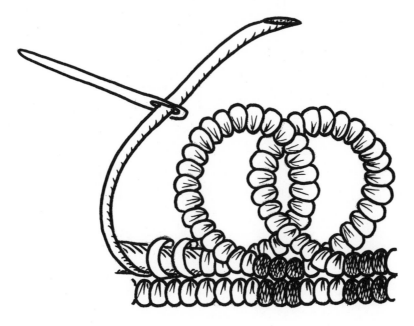

The Intertwined Cycloids, Step 1. Complete and fasten the first coil down to the previous row. Measure enough core to complete the row and cut off the core. Make the second coil. Thread the core and the needle and wrap through the front of the previous coil. Pull through.

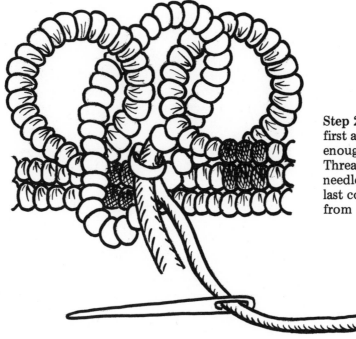

Step 2. When the sides of the first and last coils meet, wrap enough core for another coil. Thread the core and the needle and wrap through the last coil and then the first coil from the front as shown.

Continuing the Basket Beyond a Cycloid Row. Place the tapered end of a new piece of core on top of the first cycloid coil as shown. Make three continuous figure-eights. Wrap enough core to reach the second coil and fasten down. At the end of the row hold the tapered core together with the core and continue working as usual.

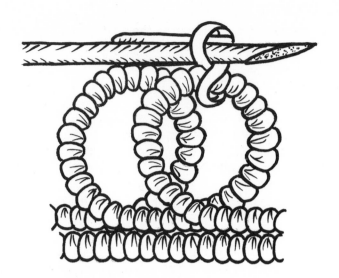

coil for this technique. Wraps may have to be added or removed after threading through and before fastening down.

Step 1. Place the coil on the previous row, tighten the wrapping on the core, and fasten down with three continuous figure-eights. Continue working the row in the same way until the sides of the first coil and the last coil meet.

Step 2. Wrap the core and place it through the last coil from the front and then through the first coil from the front. Bring the core forward between the two coils and fasten down with three continuous figure-eights. Taper the end and finish off in the usual way.

When following the above instructions, the surface result is convex. If the same directions are reversed by threading through from the back each time before fastening down, the surface will be concave. A completely different look can be achieved this way.

Continuing the Basket Beyond a Cycloid Row. After finishing the cycloid row, taper a new piece of core. Following the illustration, place the core on top of the first coil with the taper cut extending beyond the fastening point toward the working hand. Place a piece of wrap on the core and make three continuous figure-eights on top of the coil. Wrap the core until you reach the top of the second coil. Hold the core and the second coil together, and fasten with three continuous figure-eights. Continue the row in this manner until you reach the tip of the unwrapped taper of the core. Hold the tapered end and the core together, and wrap the pieces together as you finish the row. Continue with the basket using the desired weave. The cycloid has now become a decorative row in the body of the basket.

Cycloids as a Decorative Edging. Any of the three cycloid techniques can be made continuously throughout the row for the top edge of the piece. The coils may be placed in groups along the edge as well. They can be used as decorative handles when placed in groups of one or more at each side of the basket edge. When the coils are placed in groups, the areas between the coils are woven in the usual way with the figure-eight weave, stopping and starting the coils when desired. Other weaves can be used between the coils for an attractive edging. The knot and lace weaves are beautiful when used in this way.

FILIGREE LOOPING

A simple technique that is similar to the cycloids will produce an open-work effect in the basket. This technique can be put to many uses. It is easy to do, but needs careful planning and measurement to complete properly. The first project in Chapter 4 used this technique around the edge of the basket.

The loops can be open or closed, close together or far apart. They can be tall or short, rounded or squared. They can be used alternately with cycloids. They can be used along the edge or in the body of the basket. Although the variations seem endless, the general directions will be given as two groups: open loops and closed loops.

As mentioned in the cycloids, in any openwork technique it is important to wrap the core tightly and keep the wraps pushed together. If this is not done, spaces appear when the core is bent. Also, since the fastening back is the "glue" that holds a basket together, it is the most important point of all. So, fasten tightly and often while working in the openwork parts of the basket. Filigree looping also requires strong wrapping material without elasticity.

Planning and Measuring. The illustration shows some filigree looping pattern ideas. You can choose a pattern or make up your own design. The loops used in the body of the basket can be flattened into squared shapes if they are fastened securely at the top and bottom.

Measure the circumference of the basket row. Then divide the row into quarters and mark these divisions with contrasting wrap. Usually it is best to use the eye to judge most divisions in basketry, but division by measurement is quite satisfactory for these techniques. Now break down the quarters into individual areas. Keep the markers at the same place in each division (for example, all the markers are placed at the takeoff point or at the center position of the loop). You can develop a personal marking system you prefer.

An alternate method is the cartoon used in weaving. Decide on the height of the loops to be made. Cut a piece of graph paper wider than the height of the loops and the length of the circumference of the basket. Make a design plan on the graph paper to scale. Remember that the height of the loops must be decreased slightly as the row progresses so the first and last loops are the same height. Fasten the graph paper on to the row with pins when the loop is to be placed on the previous row. Form the loop around the graph paper pattern. This will keep the design even without markers.

Making Open Loops. Make three continuous figure-eights at the lift point line. Wrap enough of the core to make the entire loop. Wrap the core tightly and push the wraps together to eliminate wrap separation when the core is bent. Hold the loop in the desired shape and fasten the descending leg down to the previous row with 3 or more continuous figure-eights (see illustration). If the bottom arch is narrow, 3 figure-eights will be enough, but if the arch is wider, use the number needed to fasten it to the previous row. Wrap another section of core for the next loop. Shape, place and fasten it to the previous row in the same way as before. Continue around the row in the same manner.

The loops will remain rounded on top until the next row is added. Then the arches can be squared if desired.

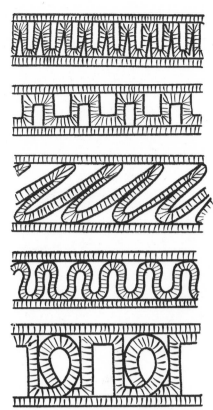

Filigree Looping Designs. There are many possibilities for design patterns in Filigree Looping.

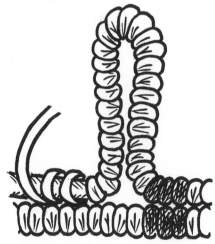

Making Open Filigree Loops. Make three continuous figure-eights. Wrap enough core to make the planned loop. Place on the previous row and fasten down with the needed number of continuous figure-eights to make the planned shape for the pattern.

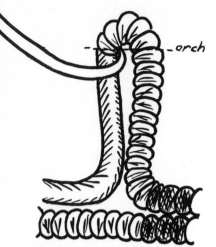

Making Closed Filigree Loops, Step 1. Wrap enough core to complete the arch on top of the loop.

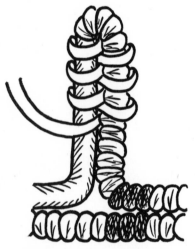

Step 2. Weave continuous figure-eights over the area to be closed. If any part of the loop is to be left open, wrap the descending leg in that area. At the base of the descending leg, fasten the core in place with the number of continuous figure-eights needed for the planned shape.

Making Closed Loops. First make the three continuous figure-eights.

Step 1. Wrap enough core for the ascending leg and the arch of the loop.

Step 2. Work in continuous figure-eights below the arch, attaching the descending leg of the loop to the ascending leg. The bottom arch is made in the same way as the open loops according to the pattern chosen.

All or part of the loop can be closed off in this manner. If the top of the loop below the arch is to be left open, wrap the descending leg down to the point where the loop is to be fastened together. If an open slit is desired on the lower part of the loop, fasten the top of the loop together and wrap the core for the remaining distance to the base of the descending leg.

Finishing Off the Filigree Looping. If the loops are rounded, taper off the core as in the cycloids so the taper lies on the lower part of the ascending leg of the first loop. If the loops are squared, taper the core so the tip ends before the corner angle of the first loop.

Finish off the row in the same way as with the cycloids. Make the taper area pleasing to the eye.

Adding the Next Row. After finishing the row, taper the end of a new piece of core. Place the core on top of the first loop. Lay the wrap on the core and fasten it with three or more continuous figure-eights. The number of figure-eights are determined by the width of the loop. Shape the loop into the desired rounded or squared form while fastening. Tightly wrap enough of the core to reach the next loop, and repeat the fastening process. Continue working the row in the same manner until you reach the tip of the taper cut.

Holding the taper end and the core together tightly, treat them as one piece until the taper is covered. Continue with the next row in the planned weave.

When fastening the top row to the loops, the work must be tight and firm to give the basket strength. Shape the loops to keep them straight and in position. Smooth the top row as well. The looping row will have to be adjusted for several rows before it will keep its proper position.

IMBRICATION

The word imbrication means an overlapping of materials. In nature the scales of a pine cone are imbricated. In fact, one traditional type of basket imbrication comes from an area of North America where pine cones are prevalent.

The final weaves in this chapter are imbrications or surface techniques for coiling and plaiting. All the techniques are worked on the surfaces of the previously finished rows.

Coiled Imbrication. The materials used for this technique include single strand yarns, doubled strands laid parallel to each other, laces, ribbons, or braids. Fabric or leather strips cut the width of or a tiny bit wider than the row can be used. These materials should be of contrasting colors to the basic basket surface to show up well.

Coiled imbrications can be added as a single interest area on the basket, or the entire basket can be imbricated.

THE BEADING WEAVE

In beading, a piece of contrasting material is laid flat on the previous row and fastened down with the next row so bits of color sparkle through the fastenings in a way that resembles beads.

Estimating Material for a Basket. If you want to use one continuous piece of fabric for the beading weave, estimate the length of the largest circumference of the basket. Wrap a piece of core to determine the diameter for the row height. Estimate the basket height, and multiply the number of rows by the circumference to get an estimate of the linear length. To estimate the length needed for looped beading, multiply the entire length by three to allow for the loops.

Making the Beading Weave. Four wraps before the lift point line, place the decorative material on the surface of the previous row.

Step 1. Make four continuous figure-eights to fasten down the end of the material. This will keep the end from loosening and will cover the cut end.

Step 2. Now wrap the core three times. Hold the material flat against the basket and fasten down with a figure-eight. Continue working in the figure-eight weave in the usual way, allowing a short strip of the contrasting material to show through in the spaces formed between the fastenings of the figure-eight weave. Wrap the core the number of times necessary to keep the spaces the same size. The number of wraps depends on the size of the wrap material.

The spaces between the fastenings can be adjusted to show more or less of the decorative material. To show longer lengths, lay the decorative

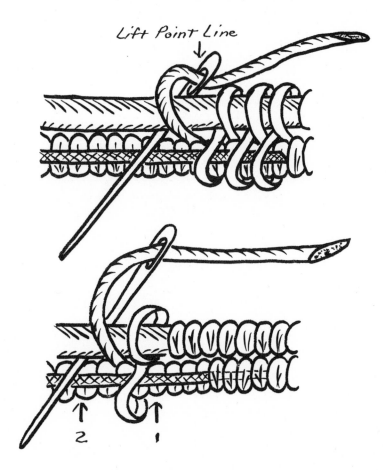

The Beading Weave, Step 1. Place the decorative material on the previous row at a point four wraps before the lift point line. Fasten the end in place with four continuous figure-eights.

Step 2. Wrap the core three times and make a figure-eight fastening over the decorative material.

material aside and continue the figure-eight weave one or two times. Replace the decorative material on the basket surface and fasten with a figure-eight. Repeat this sequence for the desired pattern. Short and long lengths can be made as well.

An interesting variation of the beading imbrication is made by pulling the beading strip into a loop before the fastening is tightened against the basket surface.

After the last beading area, fasten the end down with four continuous figure-eights. Be sure the length of the decorative material is long enough to complete the entire row. If large areas are being covered, splicing may have to be done, but it is easier not to splice unless absolutely necessary.

Adding New Decorative Material. If splicing is necessary, leave enough on the end of the piece of decorative material for a beading area, plus enough to be covered by four figure-eight fastenings. Cut off any excess. Leave the wrap hanging on the core row because it will not be used right now.

Step 1. Thread an extra piece of wrap on a needle. Needle under the wrap of the decorative row, starting about 1" (2.54cm) over on the working hand side and coming out at the point where the next figure-eight fastening will be. Pull the wrap through just until it disappears under the wraps of the row.

Step 2. Now place the end of the new piece of decorative material face down at the end of the old piece. Wrap around the decorative row four times until the ends are covered tightly. Needle through under the wraps ahead of the ends on the decorative row about 1" (2.54cm), pull through, and cut off.

Step 3. Now fold the decorative material down flat and crease it with your fingernail to flatten the fabric as much as possible. Pick up the original wrap and continue the figure-eight weave, making sure the first figure-eight fastening lies solidly over the splice joint. This will hide the splice well.

THE PLEATED WEAVE

The Klikitat Indians worked with roots and barks to produce this weave until their hands were cut and bleeding. If this basically slow technique seems to progress at a snail's pace compared to other weaves, remember that all we lose today is a little time, and the result is certainly worth the extra effort.

Traditionally, the pleated weave was folded and fastened only one time. Natural materials would stay in place because the materials themselves would not release after being folded. With soft contemporary materials, the pleating can work loose or be pulled out without a second fastening, and this extra fastening is well worth the effort because the resulting look is quite beautiful.

To estimate the amount of material needed, follow the directions for estimating looped beading.

Step 1. Fasten down the decorative material in the same way as the beading weave. Determine the length of the pleats or folds desired. Lay the decorative material flat and hold in place. Wrap the core to the first pleat point.

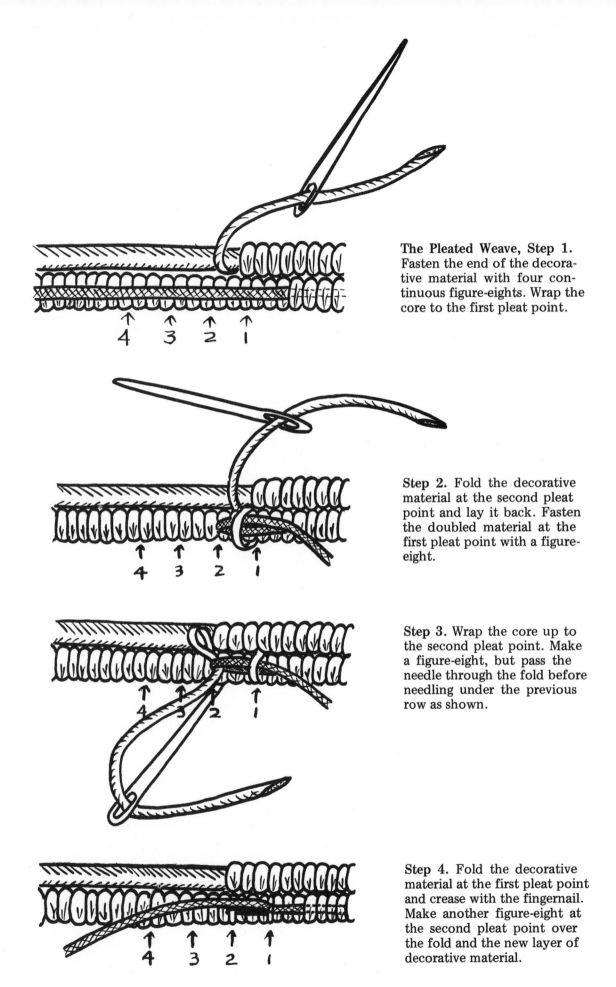

The Pleated Weave, Step 1. Fasten the end of the decorative material with four continuous figure-eights. Wrap the core to the first pleat point.

Step 2. Fold the decorative material at the second pleat point and lay it back. Fasten the doubled material at the first pleat point with a figure-eight.

Step 3. Wrap the core up to the second pleat point. Make a figure-eight, but pass the needle through the fold before needling under the previous row as shown.

Step 4. Fold the decorative material at the first pleat point and crease with the fingernail. Make another figure-eight at the second pleat point over the fold and the new layer of decorative material.

Adding New Decorative Material, Step 1. Lay the wrap material and needle aside, but do not cut off. Needle a new piece of wrap under the wraps on the previous row four wraps from the end of the piece of decorative material as shown. Pull through.

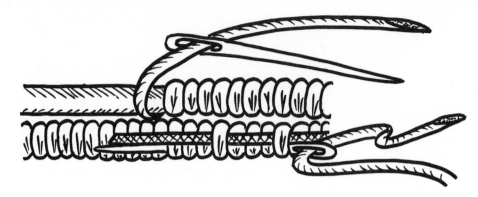

Step 2. Lay the new piece of decorative material face down on top of the old piece with the ends touching. Wrap around the previous row four times covering both ends of the decorative material and needle under the wrap, pull though and cut off.

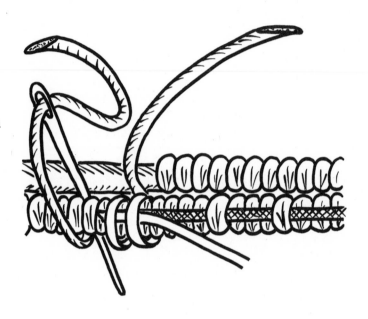

Step 3. Make a figure-eight fastening over the splice of the two pieces of material as shown.

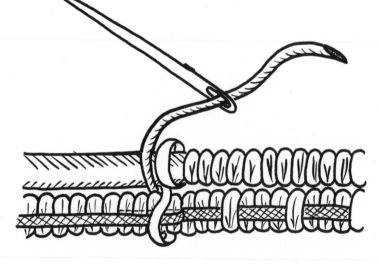

Step 2. At the second pleat point, fold the decorative material back and crease with the fingernail. Wrap the core enough times to reach the first pleat point, then make a figure-eight fastening.

Step 3. Leave the decorative material in this position and wrap the core enough times to reach the second pleat point. Make another figure-eight fastening at this point, but needle through the fold of the decorative material before needling under the previous row.

Step 4. Fold the decorative material forward from the first pleat point, creasing with your fingernail to flatten it. Find the third pleat point. Fold the decorative material back at this point. Make another figure-eight fastening over the top of the decorative material at the second pleat point. Wrap the core up to the third pleat point and needle through the fold and fasten below the previous row as before. Continue repeating Steps 2, 3, and 4 throughout the pattern area. Fasten down the end of the decorative material in the same way as the beading weave.

Adding New Decorative Material. As in beading, the material can either be taken from a continuous piece or it can be spliced. The splicing in this technique is done in the same way as Steps 1 and 2 of the beading weave splice. When splicing is done, the pleating weave should be in Step 4 of the weaving sequence. After the pieces are fastened to the decorative row, continue the pleating weave with Step 2. When you reach Step 3 of the pleating sequence again, needle through the space between the old and new pieces at the splice instead of the fold before needling below the previous row.

DECORATIVE PLAITING TECHNIQUES

The smooth and low-keyed look of plaiting can be made more exciting when you add some decoration. This extra surface technique gives a bas-relief effect to the plaited basket. The decorative row can be added at the same time as the lower row or just before the basket edge is finished. If added later, there is a more secure surface on which to work.

The overlapping row is twisted in such a way that it is lifted away from the surface of the basket to make designs or special effects. These designs work especially well on lids or basket sides. Although the same basic basket material is used, using this technique makes a plain basket look quite different.

Estimating the Length of the Material. Make a sample twist to determine the extra amount of material needed for the decorative weave. Multiply that extra amount by the number of twists planned for the row. Add that extra amount to the length needed for the woven row.

Low Twist. The low twist weave is done by twisting the weaver a complete turn to the right or left before weaving it under the next warp strip. Designs can be made with the low twist. If the designs are planned on graph paper, they can be worked out on the surface of the basket by following the graph paper design.

Using an orange stick, lift the woven material to allow the extra weaver to pass under. Twist the weaver a complete turn either to the right or left so the face of the material has returned to the front before weaving under the next row. The ends of the extra weaver are taken to the edge

Right Low Twist and Left Low Twist. This weave is done by twisting the weaver a complete turn to the right or left before weaving it under the next warp strip.

Double Twist. The weaver is turned either right or left for a complete twist and then turned for a complete twist in the other direction.

High Twist. Uses the same technique as low twist but the loop is looser and larger.

of the basket with the previous row or are spliced together at the row ends on the basket sides.

High Twist. The high twist weave is made in the same way as the low twist, except the loop is looser and larger. It requires a more rigid material to hold its shape.

Double Twist. The double twist weave is a particularly beautiful technique that can change the whole surface of the basket, make interesting areas or rows, or make an exciting lid for a simple basket.

To make the double twist, turn the weaver either right or left for a complete twist as in the low twist, (see A). Hold this twist down with the fingers and turn the weaver a complete twist in the other direction (B). Hold down the double twist and take the weaver under the next warp (C). This will hold the double twist in place. The effect of this technique is somewhat like the scale of a pine cone.

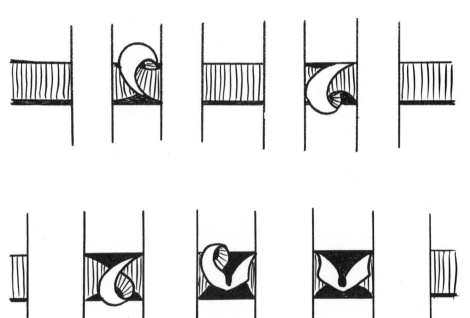

Low Twist. Lift the warps with the orange stick and slip the weaver under them until you reach the point where the twists are to be placed. Twist the weaver to the right or the left and weave under the next warp.

Double Twist. Lift the warps with the orange stick and slip the weaver under them until the design area is reached. Twist the weaver to the right. Hold down the twist, and twist the weaver to the left. Hold down both twists and weave under the next warp. This sequence places the point down. Reverse the direction for an upper point.

SAMPLE PROJECTS

Now is the time to make more sample weaves to add to your group of reference pieces. Making samples in decorative plaiting and another plaque for the coiled decorative weaves can be very helpful before starting a basket.

Project 1. Cylindrical Ripple Weave Basket. This sample was made with two different diameters of clothesline for the core. Any type of rope will do as long as the two cores have enough contrast in size to be definite and the surface of the rope is smooth. The wrap material is turquoise polyester rug yarn.

1. Taper both core ends. Place them together with core 1 on the top. Use method 2 of the circle starts. Start the basket, making sure to keep the large core (core 1) on the outside of the circle.

2. Weave four double rows of ripple weave.

3. Turning the cores slightly at the lift point, gradually lift from the basket floor so the double row 5 appears round when looking at the bottom of the basket. If this is not done, the basket will have a misshapen look.

4. Place double row 6 on top of row 5 to make the sides cylindrical. Continue weaving in the ripple weave for four more double rows to make a total of nine rows in ripple weave. Taper off core 2 and finish off core 2.

5. Work one row in figure-eight weave.

6. Add one row of filigree looping in small triangular shapes.

7. Finish off the basket.

Project 1. Cylindrical Ripple Weave Basket. Made with two different diameters of clothesline for the core, but any type of rope will do (the two cores must have size contrast and smooth rope surface). The wrap material is turquoise polyester rug yarn.

Project 2. Filigree Banded Basket. This sample basket is done with ½" (1.28cm) jute, but any rope will do. The wrap was heavyweight rug wool. Color A—orange-brown, color B—turquoise.

1. Using color A, choose a circle start and weave the basket in figure-eight weave to a diameter of about 5" (12.5cm).

2. At the lift point line, make a very slight lift. Work gently up and out for six rows.

3. Measure the circumference of the basket.

4. Plan your loop size (loop height about 1½" (3.82cm), loop width ⅞" (2.22cm)). Remember the loop decreases slightly in width as it decreases in height. You may gauge the loops by eye if desired, or plan by measurement.

5. Using color B, wrap enough core for the planned size of the simple filigree loop. Form the loop.

6. Fasten down with five continuous figure-eights. Continue the row in the same manner, keeping the loops in a vertical position from the base.

7. On the last loop, taper the core so the tip of the taper will end about halfway up the ascending leg of the first loop. Finish off.

8. Place the tapered core on top of the first loop. Using color B, fasten down with five continuous figure-eights. Wrap the core until you reach the next loop. Continue fastening and wrapping throughout the row.

9. Change to color A. Curving gently inward at the same angle as the part below the filigree looping, work one row in the pierced figure-eight and five rows in basic figure-eight weave. Finish off.

Project 2. Filigree Banded Basket. Made with jute, but any rope will do. The wrap is heavyweight rug wool. Colors are orange-brown and turquoise.

Double Wall Fur Basket. 3" x 5" diameter (7.62cm x 12.70cm). A basket created by Mary Temple as a "hand warmer, soul restorer—the bright colors of sunlight or fiery coals inside for these cold snowy Minnesota February days when we forget what the sun looks like." It is coiled over cotton clothesline with shiny rayon and wool in bright yellow, gold, orange, and brown in figure-eight weave. The basket turns down and parallels the first wall. It was difficult to work on the second wall because there was little room to manipulate the needle between the layers. (Photo by Dr. Robert Burningham.)

More Decorative Elements

6

Using just a single weave, it is possible to develop a great many types of baskets by simply changing the shaping. As new weaves are introduced, the basket forms vary even more, but by adding color, surface design, and other decorative elements, a whole new world is opened up.

These decorative additions can be simple and direct or quite complex. A beautiful feather or single colorful bead can be dramatic when placed on the proper background. Beads or shells sprinkled over the surface of a basket in a graceful pattern can be exciting. Color can make the plain surface of a basket come alive.

These additions must be chosen with thoughtfulness and care—you should have a reason for making them part of the basket. A special decorative weave is better served by one or two selected colors than chopped up with too many. Added baubles can be hidden by a busy pattern or detract from the simple beauty of a decorative weave. Remember that adding decorative elements will accent rather than cover up mistakes.

Among the possible decorative elements are: color, feathers, beads, bells, shells, fur, leather, braiding, ribbon, imitation rya knots, and surface coiling. Plaiting and twining used with coiling, and open coiled weaves used over attractive cores, can further enhance the baskets.

Think about the final use of the basket when using decorative elements. What would happen to fragile materials and objects on a working basket? Would an attractive design be more practical and make a beautiful basket as well?

COLOR

The beautiful colors we have available today are both exciting and fun to use. There are a number of ways to help yourself in choosing color combinations, and there are several ways to apply these colors to the basket.

A good color sense can be innate, but it can be learned as well. There are three ways to develop a color sense: making a color wheel, looking at designer fabrics, and observing nature (always your very best teacher).

Making a Color Wheel. The color wheel is a basic way to develop color knowledge. Although it seems like a mechanical exercise at first, if you regularly use your color wheel, an understanding of color will begin to develop. The color wheel not only shows how colors are mixed, but it shows their interrelationships. By learning to mix colors, we begin to recognize color mixes when we see them in the materials we use.

To make a color wheel, draw a large circle and divide it into 12 equal segments (see the illustration). Starting at the top of the wheel, place the primary colors as follows: (clockwise) segment 1 is yellow, segment 5 is red, and segment 9 is blue. Use paints from an inexpensive watercolor set. All of the other colors in the wheel are mixed from these primary colors.

Secondary colors are mixtures of any two primary colors. Yellow and red is orange, red and blue is violet (purple), and blue and yellow is green. If you have never mixed colors before, it is a good idea to try mixing the colors from the primary colors in the paint set. Paint in the secondary colors as follows: segment 3 is orange, segment 7 is violet, and segment 11 is green.

Next are the tertiary colors. These colors are further mixings of one primary color with one neighboring secondary color. Yellow and orange is yellow-orange, orange and red is red-orange, red and violet is red-violet, violet and blue is blue-violet, blue and green is blue-green, and green and yellow is yellow-green. These colors should be painted in order in segments 2, 4, 6, 8, 10, 12. The warm colors range between 1 and 6 and the cool colors between 7 and 12.

You can see by this intermixing that some of the colors are related and some are opposites. In using the colors together, the best blends come from using relatives together, while accents are made by using opposites.

In addition to the colors from the basic color wheel there are the neutral colors: black, white, gray, and brown. As you know, there are many shades of gray depending on the amount of white and black used in the

Making A Color Wheel. Make a circle and divide it into twelve segments. Paint in the primary, secondary, and tertiary colors as shown.

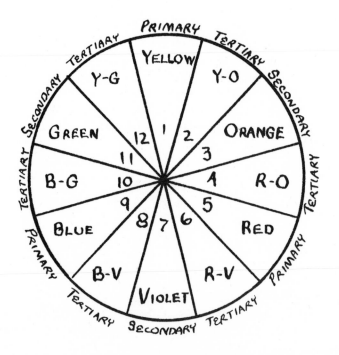

mixture. Whites can vary greatly as well, from pure white to many shades of off-white.

Browns are mixtures of one primary color with the opposite secondary color. The range of browns include: yellow and violet makes yellow-brown (tan, sand, etc.), orange and blue makes red-brown (terra-cotta, chocolate, etc.), and red and green makes dark brown (deep, muddy, etc.). Although browns are considered "neutral," they only work with related colors. But since they contain two unrelated colors, they work in two directions and will accept more colors (hence the "neutral" tag). For instance, red-brown will work with both orange and its relatives and blue and its relatives.

You can, if desired, make a larger circle than the original color wheel and paint in the different browns. Cut out the two circles and fasten them together in the center with a paper fastener. The wheels can be rotated to match the browns with their close relatives.

Use pure white with care. It can be an asset if contrast is the goal, but it can be uncomfortable to use when trying to blend colors together in a piece. For blends use an off-white.

To soften any color, add a bit of white, gray, or some other neutral color. This will give it a muted look. If several colors are being used together, two colors can be mixed at the junction between them to make the transition more gradual.

Using the Color Wheel. Here are some suggestions on ways to choose colors from the wheel:

1. Choose one color and use it in many shades from light to dark. For instance, start with a base of dark red and add lighter and lighter shades until you end with light pink at the top of the basket. The spread of color shades can be shortened (for instance: dark red to medium red, medium red to pink, etc.).

2. Vary the same color back and forth from light to dark throughout the basket.

3. Choose one color and use many kinds of textures and materials: shiny, dull, smooth, nubby, bouclé, looped, chenille, mohair, etc.

4. Choose two or three relatives on the color wheel as the main colors in the piece. Then choose an accent color straight across from the most basic color of the group.

5. Choose relatives for a gradual flow of color from one to the next without any accent color.

6. All the colors can be used if the colors move from one to the next through a relative color. This would give a rainbow effect.

When colors don't seem to work together even though you have followed all the rules, check each color you are using with related and unrelated color. For instance: gold is usually warm, but sometimes green is introduced into the dye. When gold is pulled over into the cool range this way, it can't be used with reds and oranges.

Have you ever purchased yarns only to find the color seems to have changed later? Most stores have fluorescent lighting that has a blue cast. In daylight or under the tungsten light of most homes, colors will become warmer or yellower in tone. When choosing your colors, look at them under the type of light in which they will be used. If a store has fluorescents, ask to take the material to a window or doorway to check for color.

Check all the colors you plan to use with your wheel to see how they work together. Store your yarns together in color groups and working groups. This will make it easier to find colors when you need them.

DESIGNER FABRICS

Let professionals work for you by looking at well-designed fabrics. Find upholstery and dress fabrics that have interesting color combinations. Designers are paid well to plan colors for fabrics. They have used beautiful blends that work well together. Take small swatches of fabrics with you to choose your colors. Pull off color strands from the swatches to check individual colors if necessary. Study the fabric swatches with the color wheel rules and see how they compare. If rules are broken, how? What are the results?

COLOR FROM NATURE

The finest source for color inspiration is nature. Look around you at the rocks, tree bark, flowers, leaves, sunsets, desert soils, and road cuts. Isolate the colors you see within an object or area. You will be surprised to discover some of the color combinations you will find. What is the basic color? Are there relative colors or accents? Are all of the colors bright and intense, or are some grayed, softened, or darkened?

Look at the leaves in a plant or tree. Even a bright green leaf has different degrees of color. The stems of the fuschia or red maple are brilliantly red, and this flows up into the veins of the leaves. Some trees like the camphor have new leaves of red which turn different shades of green during their lifetime only to return to the red coloring again before falling to the ground. Ask yourself what kinds of reds or greens? Do they work together? Are both bright or is one color softened? Pick up an autumn leaf from the ground and take one from a tree and study the nuances of color that from a distance become something else.

Look deeply into a flower. What colors do you see? Is there only one color or has nature combined many colors within one small nasturtium or pansy?

USING COLOR IN BASKETWEAVING

Each basketweaving technique from plaiting to coiling uses color in its own way. Plaiting uses color in the most rigid sense, while twining and coiling allow more flexibility. Colors can be planned in a design or added to a basket in a totally random way. Color can be completely independent from the shaping of the basket, or it can accent or enhance the shape.

Color in Plaiting. The use of color in plaiting is simple and to the point. Color occurs as broken lines, checks, and patterns. The color patterns are controlled by the method of weaving. Since the warps and wefts are equally visible in the weaving, the colors assume blocklike shapes and create a color study in contrasts with little opportunity for blending. There are several interesting color variations possible in plaiting:

1. Start the center with one color. Add a new color for the side wefts. This will give the base a plain look and the sides will be checked.

2. Start the center with two colors. Choose one of the colors for the side wefts. Two sides and the base will be checked while the other two sides will be one color.

3. Start the base with two colors, and choose a third color for the side wefts. This will give three completely different checked patterns on the basket.

4. Start the base with two colors and alternate these colors for the side wefts. The base will be checked and the sides will be checked and striped.

5. Do patterned weaves of plaiting in two colors to make the patterns more obvious.

6. Add one or more strips of color to the base with the warps or to the sides with the wefts for broad or narrow striped plaids.

Color in Twining. As in plaiting, all the woven patterns—such as vertical lines, checks, twills, etc.—can be emphasized with color, but more variations are possible as well. The nature of the twining process and the type of material used allows for a better blending of color.

You can add color as detailed abstract forms, as erratic twining, or as abstract color lines. Any color plan used when twining in tapestry weaving can also be used in twining baskets because the process is the same. This allows a flexibility not possible in plaiting.

Color in Coiling. The basic color elements in coiling are lines and blocks. These basic shapes can be grouped together to develop curved lines, triangles, or flowerlike designs, as well as figures of people and animals. Traditionally, these designs were used to develop personal, tribal, or religious ideas. Today we can use these same shapes to develop different aspects and ideas, and we can add asymmetrical shapes as well. In addition, we can add horizontal or vertical abstract color groupings that are very exciting and beautiful.

Since the basket is constructed in a continuing spiral, the color is either added as needed or carried along with the core to be brought to the surface when necessary. When color changes are some distance apart, the new colors are added one at a time. Colors are carried along with the core when there is only a short distance between color changes. This eliminates the problem of covering many old and new color ends. Colors that are in short supply and will be wasted by carrying them along with the core for long distances can be cut off.

SURFACE DESIGN

Color and surface design are close partners in basketry. Color can affect the design and the design can affect the color. Each needs the other to be complete.

You do not have to be able to create a picture on paper to create surface designs for basketry. Your designs can be realistic or abstract, simple or complex. Design comes from within. It is a summation of all the things you are, see, and feel. The work is an extension of you and you put part of yourself into it.

Color and design work together in nature. Flowers are designed by nature to attract insects, which perform certain functions that benefit the flower. These colors and designs are beautiful as well as useful, and they therefore attract the eye as well as the bee.

How are the colors used? Are they large solid blocks or smaller areas that seem to blend into the whole? What does the flower show at a distance, as you walk nearer, and close by? Do the lines of color encircle the flower or climb vertically up the flower sides?

As nature uses color and design to attract pollinating insects to a flower, you can use color and design to attract attention to the basket-form.

SURFACE DESIGNS IN TWINING

Plan your designs on graph paper or work them out from a mental picture as the basket progresses. Any shape can be used in the design, but curved lines produce a stepped edge as in any weaving process. Designs on graph paper flatten out as they are twined into the basket due to the differences between the physical shapes of the graph paper and the twined row. Any change of the basket circumference will require a change in the design. Designs can be worked out on the basket in different ways.

If only two colors are being used, follow the design plan row by row, twining with two different colored strands. Change the colors when needed with full and half twists.

Carrying Extra Color Strands Along Warps. If more colors are needed, extra strands can be carried along the warps in specific areas and exchanged with the working strands when needed in the design (see the illustration). These strands can be fastened to the warps with clothespins above the working area to keep them stationary and out of the way. Since these strands remain in one position, they are used for row and block designs only.

No adjustments are needed when using warp strands for row designs because the color used returns to the same warp position each time before being placed out of the way.

In block designs, the color moves across the design block to a new position in each row. Therefore, it is better to work out each block of color separately using twining methods 1 and 2. These blocks must be interlocked at the color junctions.

For more flexibility in block designs, needle in each new color needed, and needle out and cut off the extra strand.

Carrying Extra Color Strands Along Warps. When making block or row designs in twining, extra strands of color can be carried along the warps to be used as needed. These strands can be fastened out of the way as you work with clothespins.

Interlocking Colors with Method 1. Weave across the color block row in twining method 1. At the finished side of the design block, each row contains a pair of strands that will be used in the interlocking process.

At the finished side of the design block, drop strand B (see the illustration). Needle strand A through the lower strand of the pair from the top. Pull through and weave back under the first warp and place up. Pick up B. Needle through the top strand of the pair from the bottom. Pull through and weave back over the first warp and under the second and place up.

Interlocking Colors with Method 2. Weave across the row in twining method 2. At the finished edge of the design block, place strand B up (see the illustration). Needle strand A through the bottom strand of the pair from the top. Pull through and weave back under the first warp and place down. Pick up B. Needle through the top strand of the pair from the bottom. Pull through and weave back over the first warp and under the second and place down.

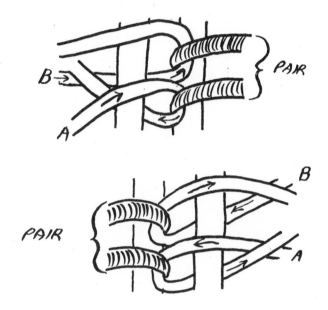

Interlocking Colors with Methods 1 or 2. After twining across the row using either Method 1 or 2, needle strand A through the top of the lower strand of the row pair weaving it under the first warp as shown. Needle strand B through the bottom of the upper strand of the row pair and weave over the top of the first warp. Now you are ready to twine back across the row using the opposite method.

Adding Color in Erratic Twining. Erratic twining is an exciting idea borrowed from tapestry weaving. It is a weaving technique that uses curved lines rather than straight lines.

To create the proper base for the curved row, areas must be shaped over which the curved lines are formed. The curved lines can be even and regular, continuing around the basket in the usual way. The curves can also be uneven and have broken lines of color if desired.

To shape the base areas, twine back and forth using twining methods 1 and 2. Drop a warp or two at the end of each row evenly or unevenly as desired. At the top of each shaped area, needle the wefts down 1" (2.54cm), pull through, and cut off. Do not allow the sides to be too steep. These areas can be the same height for the even line or different heights for the uneven line.

Abstract Horizontal Lines. Abstract horizontal lines make an interesting pattern similar to individual brushstrokes of color on a canvas. Two or three colors can be used. If three strands of color are used, two of the strands are carried in back and one in front. The colors are controlled by the use of full and half twists in almost the same way as the two-strand twining. Either of the back strands can be brought forward when needed.

Making the Full Twist with Two Back Strands. When making the full twist, treat the two back strands as a single strand.

Making the Half Twist with Two Back Strands. The half twist can be handled in two ways:

1. Do nothing to the extra strand. It moves as a floating strand from one warp to the next.

2. Half twist the back strands before the working color is brought forward to half twist with the front strand. This fastens the back strand at each warp row. If the basket is open and the inside is visible, handle the inside colors carefully to make them as attractive as the outside colors.

SURFACE DESIGN IN COILING

The development of color design in coiling is horizontal or vertical using lines and blocks of color. These shapes are grouped together to create many interesting forms that can be either realistic or abstract. The color junctions can be smooth or feathered.

Horizontal Color Patterns. If you look at the illustration you can see a horizontal line can mean a number of things. It can be one or more lines of one color in a larger body of another color. It can be the dividing line between two bodies of color. It can be rows of different colors building on top of each other. It can be long and short dashes of different colors overlapping each other at random.

A horizontal line can be bent into angles as a single line of color or as the base of a body of color.

Horizontal blocks can be used alone, floating in a body of another color, or they can be used as building blocks to create other shapes. A group of blocks can form steps, flowers, people, or other realistic or abstract shapes.

Blocks can vary in size and shape. The shape of the block can be altered to make triangles, diamonds, and other design forms. Blocks can be used to make curving lines of color on the basket surface. Small blocks stair-stepping up the basket create a spiral (see Project 2 in Chapter 4). Several of these spirals will form spokes or winged shapes. Other arrangements will make arches, flower petals, or free flowing design elements. These spirals can also be zigzagged back and forth for a change of design.

The edges of both the lines and blocks can be smooth and straight or feathered. The smooth lines are achieved by using the pierced figure-eight weave, and the feathered edges are made by using weaves that cross over the previous row of color. The traditional wrap weave will give a slightly feathered edge, but not quite as pronounced as the other wrap weaves because the crossovers are closer together.

The larger the core of the basket, the more prominent the design elements.

Vertical Color Patterns. Stripes and flowing lines can be achieved with vertical color patterns. Stripes are made by changing the colors at the

Surface Design in Coiling. Surface designs in coiling are achieved with lines and blocks of color, which can be used to develop many shapes and forms.

Erratic Twining. Twine back and forth across the row dropping off warps at each edge until a raised area has been shaped on the warps. Needle down at the top and cut off. Using contrasting color, twine over the raise to make a curved line.

Abstract Horizontal Lines in Twining. A second color can be brought forward to be twined the desired length using half and full twists. The lines are not patterned or continuous.

Uneven Vertical Triangles in Coiling. Two colors can be carried along at the same time, wrapping the unused color with the core, exchanging the colors when desired. The edges of the color stripes can be even or uneven. The triangles can be the same or a different length. These shapes can be developed into flower petals.

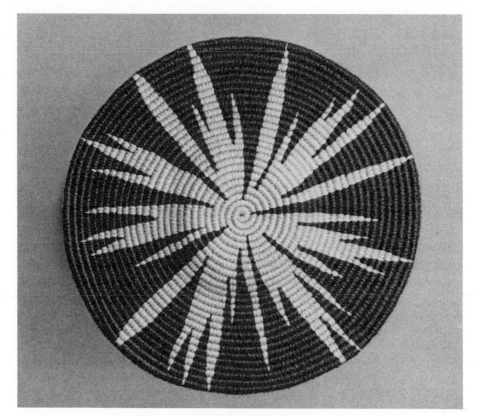

Vertical Stripes in Coiling. This basket, "Dripping Color" 5½" x 4½" diameter (13.97 cm x 10.80cm), uses the vertical stripe. It can help to disguise the tilt of the cylindrical shape. This piece is gold and brown mohair woven over jute using the basic figure-eight weave.

same time in each row. They can be narrow or wide. Stripes help to disguise the "Leaning Tower of Pisa" look in cylindrical baskets. Stripes can move spirally by picking up the stripe color just before or just after the last color change in the row. A zigzag effect can be made by changing the direction of the spiral.

Another vertical effect is made by dropping off one wrap at each side to decrease a color, or picking up one wrap at each side to increase the color area. These color areas can be closed off as triangles or left open for diagonal line effects.

An uneven flowing line, like dripping wax or flowing water, can be created by dropping off or picking up uneven numbers of wraps along the color edges. These shapes are closed off completely at the ends and create triangles of different lengths and widths. This technique is quite beautiful.

DECORATIVE SURFACE ELEMENTS

Add extra elements to your basket surface only if the addition will enhance the piece. Both the basketform and the decorative element have merit, and each must complement the other.

As mentioned before, a basket cannot be saved by the addition of a bauble or a bead. A little rya here and there can sometimes help to disguise a shape, but you shouldn't depend on these elements to cover mistakes (try to correct them if you can). Mistake baskets make good samples to keep and study, and they can be useful at the same time. Strange little shapes make great holders for paper clips, rubber bands, hair pins, pencils, and other odds and ends. These baskets can remind you of your humbler beginnings as well.

Some of the extra decorative elements that can be used are: beads, bells, shells, feathers, fur, and rya. This chapter will also include several new kinds of decorative techniques not discussed before: plaiting and twining techniques used with coiling, surface cycloids, surface coiling on finished baskets, and open coiled weaves.

Beads, Bells, and Shells in Plaiting. As mentioned before, bells and beads can be added both as edging and lid decorations. Shells can be used the same way.

Beads, Bells, and Shells in Twining. Add these objects to the surface of the basket whenever desired by threading them on the weft and placing them while weaving. Add them along the edges of the basket in the same way.

If you are making a twined piece that uses many yarn strands for the warp, the ornaments can be threaded in several ways:

1. Thread on to one to three warp strands before they are needled under the end twining for the fringe.

2. Place on the warp during the weaving process.

3. Tie on to the fringe using overhand knots.

Beads, Bells, and Shells in Coiling. Add your ornaments as the work progresses. Thread each object on the wrap as needed and wrap into place. Slip the next wrap under the object and pull especially tight to insure

Adding Shells. The openings on one side of this coiled basket called "Shell Shower" 5" x 6" diameter (12.70cm x 15.24cm) push the alignment upward unevenly to force the mouth to one side. The white pointed shells are scattered around the mouth contrasting with the bright shiny red of the synthetic wrap. This piece is an abstraction of a sea anemone. The weave is basic figure-eight.

126

good coverage of the core. If the wrap remains loose, the hard edge of the object can wear through the wrap.

If you add ornaments after a piece is finished, use strong material like waxed linen to fasten them securely.

Feathers. Add feathers to coiled baskets or along the wrapped edges or fringes in twined baskets. There are three steps required: placement, preparation of the feather, and fastening the feather on to the basket.

Step 1. A feather has two parts: the barbs and the quill or shaft (see the illustration). Place the feather on the basket to find the proper position. Arrange the feather with the barbed end toward the working hand. This makes it easier to handle and helps to eliminate tangling in the barbs. Place the quill end parallel to the core or wrap. Do not try to bend the feather into an unnatural position. A feather will return to its natural position when it is wrapped, and forcing it can break the quill. It is better to choose another feather that will curve in the proper direction.

Step 2. The best feathers for baskets are small ones, but they have very short quill ends. Since the feathers need to be wrapped on to the basket tightly, the quill of the feather needs to be lengthened or the end will pull loose from the wrap. Leave the barbs on the quill. If you remove them, you also remove part or all of the quill surface, and this weakens and often breaks the feathers. Before wrapping the feather on to the basket, dampen your fingers and twirl the quill end of the feather. Twirl until you have enough of the barbs twisted tightly against the quill to wrap the feather between six and twelve times. The number of wraps is determined by the size of the feather. The larger the feather the more wraps needed.

Step 3. Place the feather back in position and wrap on to the basket starting at the end closest to the barbs. Wrap tightly enough to keep the feather in place, but not so tight that the quill is broken.

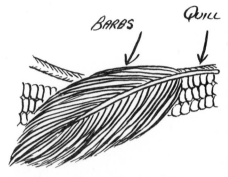

Feathers. The feather consists of two parts: the barbs and the quill (or shaft).

Feathered Nest. 3" x 8½" x 10" diameter (7.62cm x 21.6cm x 25.40cm). This coiled piece is waxed natural linen over jute with grouse feathers. The weave is basic figure-eight.

Great care must be taken when working around feathers. Try not to allow the wrap to tangle or damage the delicate feathers. Before tightening each wrap, check to see if the barbs are tangled. If so, pull them loose very carefully with the tip of the needle. Hold them out of the way and pull the wrap tight.

Caution: It is important to remember when wrapping feathers to needle from the basket toward the feather. Needling from the feather into the basket carries the barbs into the basket, and they are very difficult to extricate without tearing. You may have to change your wrapping direction to allow for this throughout the feather section of the basket.

This is not a speedy operation. Work slowly and carefully. When you are finished, dampen your fingers with very light oil (sewing machine oil is good) and stroke or preen the feathers into position. If they are broken off now, they can't be replaced easily.

Fur in Plaiting. Fur is a beautiful addition to plaited pieces. Some of the same problems encountered with feathers are found when working with fur.

Flat fur is woven in the usual way, but if it is fluffy, it can be handled in two ways. One way is to weave in the fur in the usual manner, either horizontally or vertically, pulling the trapped hairs loose with a blunt needle or pointed stick.

The second way allows all of the fur to be seen. Cut fur strips the width of the basket material. The strips should be 1" (2.54cm) longer than needed for the row. Thread a tapestry needle with waxed linen in a color that closely matches the fur. Glue the end of the thread and slip under the warp nearest the proposed fur row. Allow the glue to set, and needle through the adjacent hole between the woven strips to the front. Pull through. Place the end of the fur strip 1" (2.54cm) from the linen thread. Slip the needle under the fur hairs but on top of the hide and pull the thread across the fur strip carefully. Needle through the hole at the other edge of the strip and pull through to the back. Move over to the adjacent hole and repeat the sequence again. Continue repeating this sequence throughout the row until you are within 1" (2.54cm) of the end of the strip.

Skive or trim off the fur at one end of the strip the length of the splice. Skive the backs of both pieces at the splice area. Glue the piece, tighten the row, fasten together, and let set. Finish the row as before. Fasten the linen thread with glue under an adjacent warp inside the basket and cut off.

Fur in Twining. I do not suggest that you use fur in twining because the strips must be narrow in order to be twisted and they are too easily broken.

Fur in Coiling. Cut the fur into strips the width of the core row. Make the strips the length of the row circumference, if possible. Place a strip on the row *below* the previous row, with the hairs hanging down. Hold the fingers over the fur to keep it from tangling in the wrap.

Using a sharp needle, catch the hide 1/8" (3.175mm) down from the top when fastening back with a figure-eight. Before tightening the wrap, check to see if any of the fur has become tangled. If so, pull out the delicate hairs carefully with the tip of the needle.

Three Silver Pieces. (from top) *Silver Jinn Bottle.* 13½" x 6¼" diameter (34.29cm x 15.97cm); *Silver Pitcher.* 10" x 9¼" diameter (25.40cm x 23.49cm); *Silver Filigree Dish.* 1½" x 12" x 10" deep (3.81cm x 30.48cm x 25.40cm) These pieces are from the Silver Collection. All are made with the gray goat hair–synthetic mix over jute. The bottle has overlaid rows and a stopper of wool–lurex mix. The pieces are examples of filigree looping, sculptural design, and freeform openwork. The handle of the pitcher is an extension of the pitcher itself. The dish has a row of lace weave inside the looping.

Squash Blossom Necklace.
(right) Coiled necklace created by Teri Obole, a fiber artist from Garden Grove, California. She used waxed rayon thread for the core and pearl cotton for the wrap. The design was chosen from several Navaho necklaces. It is woven in basic figure–eight and the patterned wrap weave. The twists are fabricated onto the Naha.

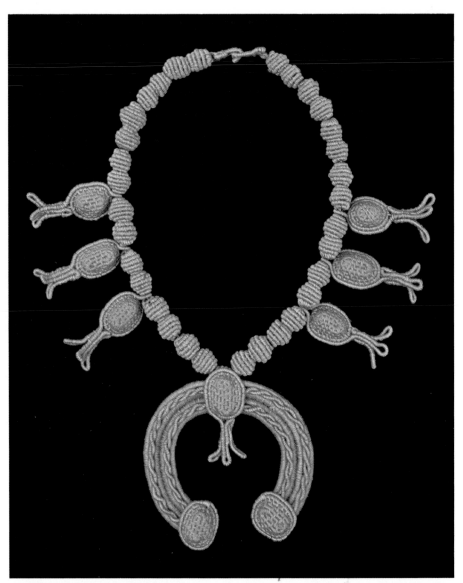

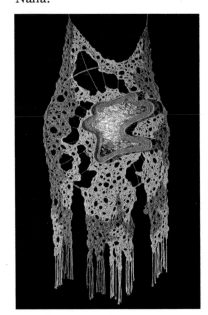

Tesserae Weaving "Torn."
(above) 11' x 4' (3.35m x 1.22m) A fiber structure woven in knotless netting over a yarn and steel armature. The bright blue resin inlay is framed by coiled basketweaving in basic figure–eight weave. The material is gray goat hair, and gray goat hair–synthetic mix.

In Russet Mantle Clad.
(right) 8" x 12" diameter (20.32cm x 30.48cm) A classic basket from her sun/fire series was created by Mary Temple of St. Paul, Minnesota. It was woven in figure–eight weave with rug wools over a nylon core, using her method of making rya. A snitch (lark's head knot) is made on the core, then pushed tightly against the previous work followed by a figure–eight. This basket appeared in *Midwest Crafts Magazine* (S'74).

Clarence. 5" x 8" x 13" deep (12.70cm x 20.32cm x 33.02cm) Clarence is coiled in figure-eight weave with rug wools and a variegated wool over jute. The variegated color gives him a speckled look. Separate pieces of the top shell are are fastened together with a single core. The legs and top shell are pushed into position by the cross structuring of the lower shell.

Mandala Shield. (above) 35" x 20½" x 5" deep (88.90cm x 52.07cm x 12.70cm) This coiled wall hanging is made of domestic and Pakistani handspun wools with five pieces of jute for the core which separate and are wrapped at the side. It is woven in basic figure–eight.

Murphy. 15½" x 8" x 12" deep (39.37cm x 20.32cm x 30.48cm) I enjoy working in my garden. Every summer, my friend the tomato worm and I square off to see who will control the family tomato crop. It has been through this lengthy relationship I have developed a hardy respect for this amusing fellow, therefore—Murphy. Heavy synthetic rug yarn and mohair over a jute core, he is coiled in basic figure–eight.

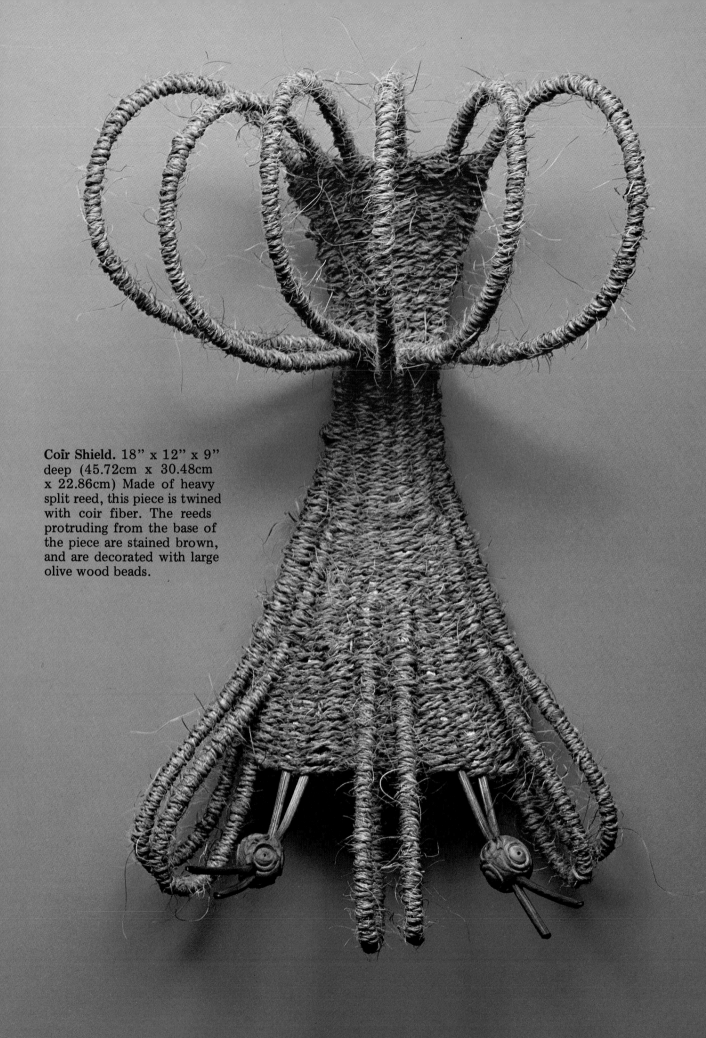

Coir Shield. 18" x 12" x 9"
deep (45.72cm x 30.48cm
x 22.86cm) Made of heavy
split reed, this piece is twined
with coir fiber. The reeds
protruding from the base of
the piece are stained brown,
and are decorated with large
olive wood beads.

It's a Fur Piece. 3½" x 8" diameter (8.9cm x 20.32cm). This little coiled piece is made in brilliant colors of yellow and orange covered with mink-dyed rabbit. The weave is the basic figure-eight, and the fur is attached with this same weave using a sharp needle. The strip is held below the previous row catching the top of the hide ⅛" (.32cm) down from the edge. This piece is to be incorporated into a wall hanging.

Fur in Plaiting. Fur can be added to a plaited piece by weaving in the usual way. It also can be added laying the strip on the basket surface and weaving a waxed linen thread over the hide under the fur hairs at each intersection of warp and weft.

If you have to add to the length of the fur within a row, place a new strip of fur tightly against the end of the last strip without overlapping and continue the row. The hairs will cover the junction if the strips are placed properly.

Position the rows of fur close enough together so both the cut edges of the strips and the basketry rows are hidden between the fur pieces. The number of basketry rows between the strips will vary according to the length of the fur hairs.

To give the top edge of the basket a finished look, take two strips of fur and place them fur sides together. Fasten the top edges of the strips with an overcasting wrap using a fine waxed linen thread. If the top edge of the basket curves in or out, the convex side of the curve will require more material to cover. Make the piece for the convex side a little longer, and as you overcast the edge, ease the longer side into slight gathers to allow a little more space.

Finish off the basket in the usual way. Place the overcasted seam on the finished edge of the basket. Using basket wrap or linen thread, fasten in place. Pull the bottom edges of the fur strips apart, pulling one strip over into the inside of the basket edge. Stroke all the fur down to smooth it. Use the tip of the needle to pull out any hairs that may be caught in the seam.

Rya. Although this technique looks like rya knotting, it is slightly different. It can be used as an accent or to further develop the shaping of the basket in twining and coiling. Rya gives a smooth flowing line to a design.

If a definite plan for the rya areas is known while the coiled basket is being woven, blanket weave ridges can be made in the areas where the rya will be placed. Rya can then be needled under the ridges after the basket is finished.

Making Rya. After the basket is finished, thread a curved needle with three or four strands of weft or wrap material. (Using several strands will make the fastenings very tight and the strands will not pull out.)

In twining, needle through under the weft next to, or through, the warp. In coiling, needle through around the fastenings strands between the rows, around the row itself, or under the blanket weave ridges.

To begin, pull the material through, leaving the ends extending the length desired. Hold these ends down with the holding-hand fingers, and needle through the same place and pull tight. Keeping the ends out of the way with the holding-hand fingers, needle through another place adjacent to the last. Pull the material through, catching it with the holding-hand index finger making a loop. Adjust the loop to the desired length. Hold the loop as you needle through the same place again and pull tight. Always work adjacent to the last loops, and move in the same direction. In this way you can keep the previous loops out of the way with the fingers as you work. Continue in the same way until the rya area is finished.

The loops can be left as they are, or they may be trimmed with scissors. Sculpturing the ends (cutting the loops to different lengths) can create an interesting effect on the basket surface and can affect the basket shape as well.

Puff.   3" x 3½" x 4½" diameter (7.62cm x 8.9cm x 11.43cm). The vertical stripes of this little coiled piece help to disguise the tilted leaning tower look in the cylindrical shape. The rya was added as a decorative puff to break the straight line of the basket. The material is orange and wood green mohair over jute.

COILING WITH DECORATIVE PLAITING MATERIALS

Flat ribbonlike plaiting materials can be used very effectively in coiling. Use ribbons, braids, or leathers, with filigree looping and open or closed cycloids to further decorate the baskets. You might also use fabrics, vinyl upholstery, or wrapped core pieces.

There are two types of materials to be considered: fabric and non-fabric materials. Each needs to be handled in slightly different ways. Both the width of the material and the type of pattern also need to be considered.

Using Fabrics. The cut ends and/or the cut sides of laces, braids, ribbons, and fabrics must be specially handled.

If there is no pattern, or the pattern is not prominent, measure the width of the material and plan the size of the loop or coil to accommodate it. Remember the loop and coil rows decrease slightly in height at the end. Allow the decorative material a little breathing room in the beginning, and keep it as tight as possible at the end without cramming it. Allow 1" to 2" (2.54cm to 5.08cm) extra length for splicing.

If the edges of the decorative material are cut, double the width of the material and add enough for seam allowance. Fold the material inside out and stitch the seam lengthwise by hand or machine. Turn the tube right side out and press flat, placing the seam in back.

Finish the basket before attempting to weave any decorative plaiting material, unless it would be difficult to work inside the finished basket due to a small neck or awkward angle. In this case add the material after weaving a few rows beyond the decorative row.

Weave the material through the loops or coils starting at the lift point line. Fold and overlap the ends and sew them with a hidden stitch. Stretch the decorative material tightly around the basket before fastening together. Make sure the folds are hidden under the loops or coils of the basket.

Prominent repeating patterns need planning. Measure the distance needed between the patterns and plan the loops and coils accordingly. Some of the loops may have to be closed to frame the pattern properly. Closed filigree loops may have to be used between the coils of the cycloids to achieve the right spacing.

When planning the pattern placement, remember that the distance taken up by the thickness of the wrapped core in the loops and coils must be allowed for.

Weave the patterns in their proper places. Fold the ends of the material, tighten in place, and sew together. If the inside of the basket is open, the inside seam must be hidden as well.

Using Non-Fabric Materials. The general directions for measuring and weaving leather and vinyls are the same as for fabrics. The edges, however, require no special treatment.

In splicing the strips of material, leather needs to be skived (shaved) before gluing the splice together, while vinyl can be trimmed at an angle with scissors to remove the blunt end. If vinyl has a cloth backing, remove the backing from the splice area and then angle trim with the scissors before joining.

Cylindrical Plaiting Material in a Coiled Basket. When weaving a wrapped core through loops and coils in plaiting fashion, the cylindrical cores will

1

2

3

Coiling with Decorative Plaiting Materials. There are many variables possible with this type of plaiting. Place the loops and coils far apart or close together. Make the weaving regular or irregular. Patterns 1 and 2 can be made with loops or coils. Other variations are possible with these patterns as well: skipping loops and coils or irregular groupings (2 and 3, 1 and 3, etc.). Vary pattern 3 by placing coil groups in between areas of the loose loops.

Maytime (below). 3" x 8½" x 7¼" diameter (7.62cm x 21.59cm x 18.42cm). This coiled basket was wrapped in light orange linen. The open filigree loops at the base were plaited while the ones at the top were made to change the coiling line of the basket. Several types of lavender ribbon were tried for the plaiting, but they were not right. A ribbon was woven using a lavender shade of the linen basket material.

require more space than flat materials. Measure the width of the core. Determine the height necessary to make the loops or coils big enough to receive one or two of the wrapped cores.

After finishing the row of loops or cycloids, do not cut off the core. Change the wrap to a contrasting color behind the leg of the first loop or coil. Wrap the core until there is enough to reach once or twice around the basket according to the plan for a single or double row. Fasten the wrap with a single blanket weave or half hitch at the end of the wrapping to keep it from slipping loose during the weaving process.

Measure another circumference length, plus several inches more of the unwrapped core, and cut off at a taper. Weave one or two rows of core into the loops or coils, keeping the core straight. Remove the half hitch from the end of the wrapping. You may need to add or remove some wraps at the end of the core to adjust to the space. When the end of the contrasting color is behind the last leg of the loops or coils, change to the original color. Wrap enough core to reach the top of the first loop or coil. Fasten in place with continuous figure-eights. Continue the row fastening to the loops or coils in the usual way. Finish the basket.

Smaller core can be used for this technique if desired. If so, taper the regular core at the end of the last loop or coil, and splice on the tapered end of the smaller core. At the end of the weaving process, taper the end of the smaller core, splice on the regular core, and continue the basket. The splice points should be hidden behind the first and last loops or coils. These loops can be closed if desired to cover the splices.

TWINING ON COILED BASKETS

This technique is an open twist, and can be either double or triple. Measure the circumference of the basket. Divide the distance into even divisions plus one extra space for the double twist or a number divisible by three plus one extra space for the triple twist. Mark each one of these points. These are the fastening points for the wrapped core. Make the first row like a row of filigree looping, fastening the loops at Point A (see the illustration) in either method. Now place the loops at every other or every third marked point, making sure the tops are even. When the first row is finished, measure the length of the core material required for the first row. Multiply this by three or four according to the chosen method. Cut off the core at a taper.

In making the second row, wrap enough length on the core to cross over the first loop to the front of the work. Fasten down at Point B with continuous figure-eights. Thread the core, then wrap and needle through the loop to the back. Wrap enough core to cross over to the front of the second loop to the next fastening Point B. Continue the row in the same way, making sure the tops are even.

If doing the triple twist, fasten the wrapped core at the remaining marked points (C), going in front of two loops and threading under and behind them after fastening down.

These techniques make beautiful edges. When using twining as an edge, taper the end and finish off (see the dotted line in illustration). If the twining is used as a decorative row, do not finish off. Instead carry the wrapped core over and start weaving the next row on top of the first loop (see the illustration). After making the row on top of the decorative row, finish the basket.

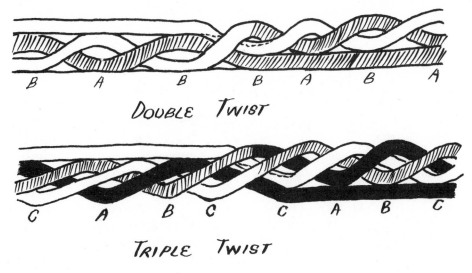

DOUBLE TWIST

TRIPLE TWIST

SURFACE CYCLOIDS

False handles or small groups of decorative cycloids can be made on the surface of the basket as the basket is woven. At the point where the coils are to be placed, make the desired number of cycloid coils, and continue weaving the row in the chosen basket weave.

In the next row before reaching the coils, make three or more continuous figure-eights to strengthen the edge. Wrap the core the length required to stretch behind the coils and fasten down with three or more continuous figure-eights on the row beyond. Continue the row as usual. The coils will tilt out from the side of the basket.

SURFACE COILING

Surface coiling can be attached to the basket with a straight or curved needle. A straight needle can be used if the inside of the basket is accessible, but if not, you will have to work on the basket surface with a curved needle.

The wrapped core must be fastened tightly to the basket as often as necessary to make a snug connection, but you can make interesting loops and coils. The coiling can be fastened into the wrapping or weaving surface of the basket. It can be attached to the fastenings between the rows or around the rows themselves. Fasten down with a wrap or figure-eight.

If the surface coiling on a basket started with an unwrapped tapered end, come back to this point to end it. Taper the end and splice it to the beginning taper. Finish wrapping the core, needle under, and cut off. Twining can be spliced together in the same way after finishing the surface design, if desired.

If you have one or more separate ends to finish off, taper the ends, coil them around, and fasten them to an existing surface piece by wrapping the two pieces together. Needle under the wrap, pull through, and cut off.

OPEN COILED WEAVING

Open coiled weaving was an important method in traditional basketry. It was fast and used less wrapping material than closed weaving. This was important to people who had to collect and prepare all the materials they

Twining on Coiled Baskets. Divide and mark the circumference into spaces divisible by two or three and add one extra space. Make filigree looping fastening the loops at the A markings. Cut the core leaving more than enough length for the chosen method. At the lift point line, place the wrapped core in front of the previous loop, and thread through under the loop after fastening down at Point B. Continue the row in the same way. In the triple twist, add the third row. Fasten the core at Point C going in front of two loops and threading under the same two loops after fastening down. At the end of both methods, taper the core and finish off (see dotted line) or continue into the next row as shown.

used. The preparation of most natural materials takes several months to a year.

In contemporary basketry it is often difficult to find an attractive core that is as strong as necessary for good open weaving. For that reason it is being included here as a decorative weave rather than as a basic weave.

To use this technique it is necessary to find materials that are strong enough to support the basket, since the open weave is not structurally sound in itself. Sisal, manila, reeds, and sea grass are available in some areas and are ideal for open coiling.

The long needles of the black pine and some other coniferous trees make attractive cores. The pine needles can be worked either green or aged. Green needles are easier to work with, and if your work is extremely tight, shrinkage is minimal. Place the finished piece in a dry, dark place to age the needles.

If you wish to age the needles before using them, put them in a paper bag in the garage. Keep the needles straight and flat. Needles aged in the dark stay green, and when they do begin to fade, remain an attractive color. Aged needles must be dampened to make them workable.

Plastic tubing is an exciting material to use in open weaves. It is like something from the space age.

Pinkie. 4" x 5¼" diameter (10.16cm x 13.34cm). A coiled basket made of sisal core wrapped with pink jute. It is woven in double open wrap weave and basic figure-eight.

Starting an Open Weave Basket. Choose any of the basket starts in Chapter 4. Work in basic figure-eight for several rows before starting the open weaves.

Use a soft material like jute or clothesline to start the basket if the material used for the basket core is too stiff to bend into a tight circle. Taper the end of the core material at a point where it will be hidden under the figure-eight weave. Splice the tapered end of the basket material on to the tapered end of the soft core. If using pine needles or reeds, add a few at a time over this tapered area until only pine needles remain before starting to weave in the open weave.

The same weaving procedure is used for a single or multiple core, except the multiple material is added a piece at a time when needed. The pieces overlap and appear to be a continuous piece of material. Pine needles can be arranged to allow one end to appear on the surface at each wrap fastening point for a special touch.

At the lift point line, needle through on the working hand side of the last figure-eight fastening and pull the wrap to the back of the work. This places the wrap in the position to wrap toward yourself in order to needle through from the front.

Single Open Wrap Weave. Starting at the lift point line, wrap over the top of the core at a 45° angle (see Row A). Needle under a strand of wrap on the previous row. Pull through to the back of the work. Continue the row to the lift point line. Keep the first row wraps close together to allow for separation as the basket increases in size. On succeeding rows fasten the wrap by needling under the single wrap on the previous row (see Row B). On the last row, taper the core at the lift point line and continue wrapping past the taper point. Now rewrap the last row over the previous wrapping, covering the core completely without fastening back to the previous row. Wrap ½" (1.27cm) past the tip of the taper cut, needle under the wrap, pull through, and cut off. This will strengthen the basket edge.

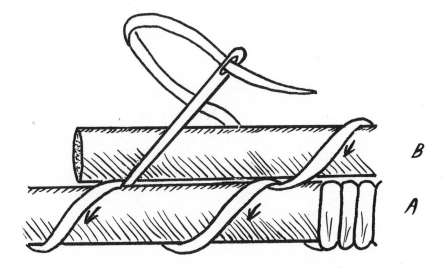

Single Open Wrap Weave. Make a round start and weave in figure-eight for 2 to 3 rows. Bring the wrap to the front. Needle around the last figure-eight fastening on the working hand side and pull through to the back. Now wrap each row as shown catching the wrap at the top of the previous row from the front (see Row A). In each succeeding row, needle into the previous single wrap from the front (see Row B).

Double Open Wrap Weave. Start the basket as before. Work the first row in single open wrap weave to the lift point line. Needle under the top of the wrap at the lift point line and reverse directions. Wrap back over the same row toward the beginning (see Row A). Cross the single wraps at the top, forming an X. Needle into the same places as the single wraps to keep the angles even.

You must adjust the wrap into working position again before beginning the next row. When you reach the lift point line, needle under the last Single Wrap on Row A. Now bring the wrap between Rows A and B to the front. Needle around the fastening at the lift point line, carrying the wrap to the back again (see the illustration). Now you are in position to begin the single wrap in the next row.

Each succeeding row is made in the same way as the second row, with two exceptions. First, fasten the wraps at the cross points on top of the previous row. Second, the starting point in each new row shifts slightly to the working hand side of the last starting point.

When you are ready to finish the basket, the row beginning may have shifted some distance away from the lift point line. If this is true, and the basket will not even out at the top edge at this point, you will need to make an adjustment by making a partial row to complete the basket to the lift point line.

Start the row and work to the lift point line in single open wrap weave. Reverse and work back to the beginning of the row. Needle under the top of the row 1" (2.54cm), pull through, and cut off. Now needle under 1" (2.54cm) on top of the row at the lift point line. Weave this row in single open weave and finish off as in the single open wrap weave.

Double Open Wrap Weave. Complete a row of single wrap weave. Now wrap back toward the beginning of the row crossing over the single wrap at the top of the row making an X. Needle into the same places as the single wrap (see Row A). At the lift point line bring the wrap forward between Rows A and B. Needle around the last fastening point to the back and pull through. Continue each row in the same way fastening the wraps at the top crossings of the previous rows (see Row B).

Nine By Seven. 7" x 9" diameter (17.78cm x 22.86cm). After making a simple oblate form, the core was wrapped to make a large coil on the top fastened at two sides. More rows were added to the coil, and then it was brought up and fastened together at the top with the last row. The weave is double open wrap weave over 8 mil plastic tubing with three strands of purple rayon weaving yarn.

Furcated Double Open Wrap Weave. Make the single wrap weave around the row. Now reverse as in the double weave. After making the first crossing, needle under the row and pull through. Bring the wrap up over the core and straight down over the front of the row to needle under the row again (see Row A). Continue the row in the same way.

In succeeding rows, the single and double wraps are fastened under the top of the straight wrap. When the straight wrap is made, needle directly into the center of the previous straight wrap, splitting it (see Row B). This forms the furcated weave.

Adding New Wrap in the Open Weave. If you run out of wrap material when you are making the single wrap, lay the end on top of the core.

Step 1. Needle the new piece of wrap under the last two wraps and continue on with the single wrap, making sure to wrap over the old end at least twice.

Step 2. If you are making the double wrap or furcated double wrap when you run out of material, needle the old wrap under the wraps in the direction you are working, and needle the new wrap under the wraps in the opposite direction. Be sure the new wrap is tucked under the working wrap to hold it in position when you make the next angled wrap, since each wrap shows up well in this weave and must be carefully placed.

Furcated Double Open Wrap Weave. After completing the single wrap weave row, reverse direction and needle under for one double wrap weave. Pull through and bring the wrap straight up over the center between the two crossings on top of the row. Needle down through the center again and wrap over the next single wrap. Continue the row in this manner to the lift point line (see Row A). Encircle the last fastening point to adjust the wrap as before.

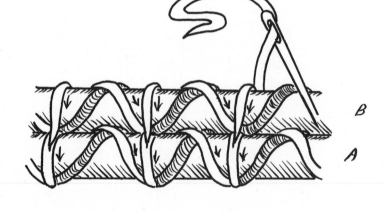

Adding New Wrap in the Open Weave, Step 1. Needle the end of the wrap under two single wrap crossings as shown.

Step 2. After needling under the last two double wrap crossings as shown, bring the wrap down over the front and needle under the row. Continue the row.

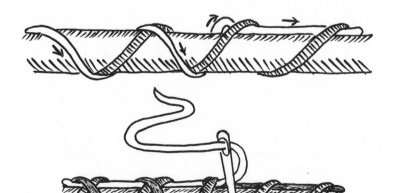

144

SAMPLE PROJECTS

For this chapter, I suggest that you make small samples of the open weaves for future reference rather than follow actual projects. The possibilities are too varied to narrow down to specifics. Good weaving, and have fun!

Open Wrap Weave Project. The upper plaque is woven in the single open wrap weave. The lower plaque is woven in the furcated double open wrap weave. The wrap is black jute over a sisal core.

Seashore Sunset. 62" x 29" x 7" diameter (157.48cm x 73.66cm x 17.78cm). Worked over a steel armature, this fiber structure includes weaving, basketweaving braiding, wrapping, macrame, knotting, and looping. The material is jute in natural colors and shades of gold to rusty orange. It is ornamented with red-orange beads, bells, and ostrich feathers. The coiled basketforms are in basic figure-eight.

Beyond Baskets

7

Two of the marvelous things about people are their individuality and versatility. If a group of people visit the deserts of Utah, each one will carry away a different feeling, a different idea, for each person looks at the world in his own way. What each person sees is influenced by who and what he is. It is these personal influences that direct one person to feel the warmth of the sun, or another to see the brilliant colors in the rocks and sand, or yet another to seek out interesting rock formations.

Give this same group of people instruction in one basketweaving technique, one weave, and identical materials, and each will produce a different basket. One might produce a classic basket, another a handbag, and still another an item to wear on the body. Others will use the technique to create artforms. In so doing, each one will receive a completely different feeling of fulfillment.

Where are you now? What are your goals? How do you plan to reach them? Do you need to stay in a secure place right now, or are you willing to forge ahead into something new? Are you a practical person who finds it difficult to create something unless it has a definite function, or are you one who creates for the sheer delight of creation?

If you do not want to leave the realm of baskets, there are endless ways to vary them. With new weaves, new shapes, different colors, and new designs and ornamentation, you can create a steady flow of beautiful baskets with endless variation.

Variations on a design theme can be an interesting study. A lifetime can be spent this way. Datsolalee, the famous Washoe Indian basketweaver, spent her life preparing excellent materials, improving her technical skills, and telling stories with her simple designs. Today, her flawless baskets stand out above all the rest.

If you want to go beyond baskets, you can still remain in the world of practical function with hair and body ornaments, miscellaneous bags, pillows, clothing, clothing ornaments, household accessories, and furniture.

If you want to venture out into the world of fanciful design, you can leave "containers" behind and use only the techniques themselves to break all traditions. Imaginative sculptural experiments can be totally abstract, or they can become a personal characterization of a familiar object. The only limitation in this journey is the limitation of the craft itself.

It is not necessary to know what you plan to do. You can simply gather materials you like and begin. Some of the most imaginative pieces evolve from this procedure. It is a sort of mindless doodling with your materials that grows and develops into something great.

BUILDING AN IDEA STOREHOUSE

Remembrances of past experiences will influence your work—places you have been, things you have seen, things you have done, even people and animals you have met. You don't have to bring the entire experience into being, only its essence—the colors of the Southwest mesa country, the curves of the ox-bow lakes along the Mississippi, the smell of the northern pine country, the mystery of the Louisiana bayous.

Textures can come from trees thick with moss or eroded rocks of the arid southwest. Surface designs might come from flowing lines of water or trees bending in the wind, the shape of an interesting leaf or a fallen pine cone. What do you see in the shape of a fuschia or a jack-in-the-pulpit? Do you remember the fairyland that last winter's snowstorms made in the barren garden outside?

Color can be taken from a canna, the roof of an ice cave, or a favorite lake.

For shaping, watch the movement of an athlete seen through the eye of the slow motion camera, a gnarled or twisted tree, the flight of a bird, a fat ripe melon, or the inching of a tiny caterpillar.

Even in the depths of the city you will see frost on the window, paint peeling from a fence, shiny new buildings reaching high in the sky, iron rust at the docks, a saucy pigeon, or the mix and flow of colors as groups of dancers flash by on television.

No matter where you are, stop, take time to look, time to absorb what you see. Take time to hear, to feel, to smell. Begin to use your senses to the fullest. Use these impressions to bring forth new expressions from you.

PUTTING THIS INFORMATION TO WORK

When moving away from simple basket construction, certain questions present themselves. How can each technique best be used? What limitations should be placed on it? Will your ideas work in basketry? What is the final use for the basket? Will it work as a completed product?

Structural principles must be followed to make the piece work. Some rules can be bent or broken if other rules are followed. Surface weaving and coiling, leaving open areas, special shaping, and other problems must be considered now.

CHOOSING THE RIGHT TECHNIQUE

To use a technique best, thought must be given to the ways each technique works. What are the special characteristics of plaiting, twining, or coiling? Which technique assumes an oblate shape best? Which works best in tall vertical pieces? Which will accept your color design best? Which technique will produce your idea in the strongest way?

If you want to combine techniques, how do you go about it? What do you do with the warp ends of the twining? How do you join the techniques together?

If you have not made samples in the technique you plan to use, do it now. Try your ideas in small pieces or samples. Don't waste your time on a large piece until you are sure it will work. If your idea doesn't work, find out why. Would it work better in another technique, another weave, another material? Are the materials unbalanced (core to wrap, warp to weft, wrap or weft materials to each other)? Are the cores or warps too rigid, too soft, too small, too large?

DEVELOPMENT OF SCULPTURAL IDEAS

People often ask how to work sculpturally. If you have been able to form a simple basket, you have made your first step in the right direction. You do not have to be a sculptor to work out sculptural pieces.

SCULPTURAL TWINING

The construction of twining is somewhat limiting as to direction, but many things can be done within the shape itself. Finish a basket center plus about ½" to 1" (1.27cm to 2.54cm) more. Grasp the warp ends and move them about to see what they will do. Stretch them tall, squash them flat, separate them, braid them.

Slits, wrapped warp, exchanged warps, braiding, and surface weaving with the warp ends are a few of the ideas that can be used.

Slits. To make slits, twine the warps up to the planned slit, reverse, and twine back around to the other side of the slit. Twine back and forth in this manner until the slit is long enough. It can be as long or short as you desire.

Wrapped and Exchanged Warps. Twine areas leaving lengths of warp unwoven. Wrap these warps separately with the same weft material or a contrasting color. Needle the ends of the wrapping into the twined areas above and below the wrapping.

Extend or pull warps out of the piece and bring them back in when desired. Take the free warps from one area and place them in another for a different look, or twine as a strap.

Braiding. Twine or wrap the separate straps or warps, then braid them before the basket is woven in the usual twining again.

Using Warp Ends. The problem of finishing warp ends on a twined basket becomes an experience in sculptural work. Fringe or use the ends as surface weaving. If you leave the warps free at both ends of the work, eliminating the basket center, these free ends can be joined in circles (see the photo on bottom of page 151).

Twining is especially good to use with vertical ideas in sculpture. Surface designs are not a visual problem in cylindrical twining as they are in cylindrical coiling.

Twining with Stiff Spines. Stiff spines can act as a base or as a decorative element within the twined piece.

Add the spines after the basket center is finished. They may protrude at the bottom of the work as a stand, end within the basket structure or protrude at the top as a decorative element. They may be wrapped, dyed or stained and used as an extension from the piece (see the color photo on page 132).

Coiled Base Extensions for Twining and Coiling. Since the twined piece has a rounded bottom, you may want an extension on the base to make it more stable. Start a coiled extension with a tapered end and work around the piece, building it up as desired. Finish off in the usual way. Make a base extension for a coiled piece in the same way (see the photo on top of page 151).

SCULPTURAL COILING

Coiling lends itself to more freedom sculpturally because it can move in any direction you desire. To use coiling you must simply learn how to alter the original basket shape.

Use the following techniques for abstract sculptured pieces as well as realistic forms.

Slits. Make slits by wrapping a length of core tightly without fastening back until the slit is as long as desired. Make other openings by wrapping lengths of core to loop up, inward, or outward from the row, or to arc across the inside edge of the basket before fastening down. In succeeding rows work around these changes to form extensions, depressions, or openings.

In making openings, always strengthen each end with a number of continuous figure-eights. Wrap very tightly around openings and on the cores that extend across or loop around the openings. Push the wraps together tightly on the core to make the wrapping stronger.

Adding Extensions. To add a piece to an opening for an extension, tube, or neck, taper the end of a piece of core and work around the opening. This becomes a new basket form attached to the main piece.

Multiple Necks. Add several necks to an existing base by wrapping the attached core the length you need to make the base of the first neck. Coil the wrapped piece around and fasten it down at the proper point on the previous row. Continue adding rows to this base until the neck can be finished off.

Add other necks, one by one, by fastening the tapered ends on to the adjacent surfaces of the base or bases of previously finished necks. Placing the tapered start on the adjacent surfaces will hide the starting pieces (see the photo on page 152). Be sure to join them with continuous figure-eights to make the joinings stronger. Make each succeeding neck as you made the first, forming it as desired.

You may have to work on the necks simultaneously because shaping or ornamentation might make later work difficult or even impossible. If this is necessary, make butterflies of the core and wrap material not being used and tuck into the neck structure.

Lengthening Areas Without Leaving an Opening. To raise one side of the

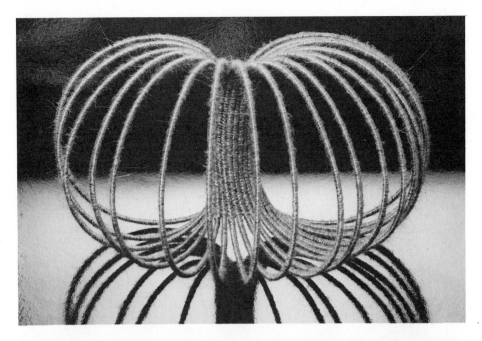

Silver Fountain. 9" x 16" x 9" diameter (22.86cm x 41.91cm x 22.86cm). This twined piece from the Silver Collection is composed of a series of circles. It is wrapped and twined with a gray goat hair–synthetic mix over reed.

Chinese Vase. 5¼" x 5½" diameter (13.34cm x 13.97cm). This coiled basket is made of Swiss straw in shades of violet and chocolate brown. The added base follows the lines of the filigree looping and duplicates the top of the basket. The weave is basic figure-eight. If baskets are used as plant holders, they must be protected from dampness. It is best to use waterproof materials.

Sparkle Plenty (above). 5½" x 4½" diameter (13.97cm x 11.43cm). The dual necks in this coiled piece are fastened together on adjacent sides. The second neck was started at the inside base of the first. The material is wool-lurex mix in magenta and blue-black over jute.

African Head (above right). 22" x 12" x 17" diameter (55.88cm x 30.48cm x 43.18cm) Black jute over a jute core, this coiled piece shows examples of ornamentation with shells, bells and beads. Separate pieces were made for the cheeks and chin and then added to the main basketform. The weave is the basic figure-eight.

sculptural piece without leaving an opening, add short lengths of core in that area. The regular core is not cut off. Add the pieces between the rows while the regular core is set aside.

When making Murphy (see the color photo on page 131), the outside curves of his body needed to keep up with the inside curve visually, and short lengths had to be added to lengthen the curves.

Taper the core pieces on both ends. Wrap the first tapered end on to the existing row until it can be worked separately without pulling loose. Weave up to the other tapered end and finish off. Do not place two added pieces of the same length together in adjacent rows. The pieces should vary in length to keep the wrapped sections from being too visually prominent. If you need two pieces the same length, add a regular row between them.

Separate Shapes. Make separate pieces to create certain shapes when these shapes cannot be made in the line of work. Then add these pieces to the main form and continue working.

Clarence's top shell is made of many little separate pieces fastened together (see the color photo top of page 131). His legs, head, tail, and lower shell were made separately and then added as well.

Certain areas of the African Head, such as the cheeks and chin, were made separately and then inserted where needed (see the top right photo on page 152).

Open Areas. In open areas, extra strength must be built in to make the piece stable. Wrap the work very tightly. Adding a second row to a loop or coil makes it stronger, but allows it to remain an open area (see the bottom photo on page 152). Making double rows by placing the second row on top or at an angle strengthens and gives a bas-relief effect.

Aladdin's Lamp. 11½" x 14½" x 4½" diameter (29.21cm x 36.83cm x 11.43cm). Coiled piece from the Scheherazade series of the Silver Collection, made of gray goat hair–synthetic mix over jute. Lid and handle decorations are extensions of the piece itself, and open areas are strengthened by doubling. Weave is basic figure-eight. figure-eight.

Making a Clay Model. If you are not sure about the shape you want to make, and how it will work out, use a lump of clay to shape into the object. Look at it carefully, and find the point where the basket center will be. Sketch the lines of the core rows with a pointed stick. Is the center an oval, a circle, a square, or asymmetrical? Sketch the lines around in the same way as you would work out a basket.

Decide at this time whether unusual spaces will be left as openings or filled in with short lengths of core. Does an area seem to require a separate piece? How will you make extensions, depressions, or other unusual shapings? Where will extra structural strength be needed?

Doodling. As mentioned before, some of the most exciting pieces of abstract work can evolve with basketry "doodling."

First, take your core and let it coil around and fall by itself. Look at the shapes. Do this a number of times until you see how the material wants to shape itself. If you see something you like, try to duplicate it as a basket.

Start out with a circle or an oval center. Make a basket base if you wish, or make several little shapes that can be incorporated into a larger piece. Build two or more rows for a base before you begin to work out some "doodling" ideas. Weave around the center, loop or coil around it or on one side, reverse direction, or work on top of the center piece spilling off on the other side in loops and coils. Follow some of the loops and coils more than once, either on top or around the edge. Let things happen. Allow the unwrapped core to loop and coil on the piece to see how it will look before you wrap and fasten.

From an ordinary basket base, work the core vertically, looping and coiling the top edge of the basket. Make the rows uneven, beside, under, or on top of each other. Leave openings and build up areas.

"Doodling" can follow lines of flowing water around and over rocks, gnarled tree bark, or twisted roots as they appear above the surface of the ground.

Begin coiling with any shape and develop it into any shape. Since the base is a single core, it can go in any direction—up, down, back, forth, in a spiral, or around the surface of the piece. It is not limited to a single space, row, or shape.

An example of the "doodling" process is Silver 2000. With a general idea of the completed work in mind, loops, coils, vertical rows, and twisting and turning in single and multiple rows were used to make up this piece (see the photo on page 154).

Educating Your Hands to Feel Shapes. Have you ever tried to feel shape? Blind people have an advantage in this. They have to learn what shape looks like by touching it. You can do the same thing, but being sighted you tend to use your hands less to distinguish shape. Hold an orange, a vase, or a pitcher. Run your hands over the object. Close your eyes, and feel the shape, the texture. Smell the fragrance. Feel a carved figure of a person or animal. Can you distinguish the shape with your fingers? Do the

Silver 2000. 11" x 17" x 11" diameter (27.94cm x 43.18cm x 27.94cm) This coiled piece is an artform of complete fantasy made with the twists and turns of "doodling." It is gray goat hair-synthetic mix over jute core woven in basic figure-eight.

154

feelings change when you close your eyes? Learn to make your hands see for you.

Take a lump of clay. Can you duplicate one of the simple shapes you have seen or felt? Compare your clay piece with the original object. Feel both. See what your touch tells you about the two pieces. What are the differences? Now take the clay and form something from your mind. Feel the bulges and depressions. Run your hands over a basket. How does it feel? What are your impressions?

Reversing and Changing Directions. A rule of basketweaving that needs to be broken in sculptural basketry is the one which tells you to work always on the outside of the basket. Since the core must be bent back upon itself at times and taken back across the row in the opposite direction, you will have to work on the inside of the basket, difficult though it can be. To do this, you must watch the shaping carefully, and give the basket extra support. Do not hold on to the weaker edges. Work slowly and carefully.

Support Aids for Working Baskets. To support a weak area in awkward positions, place something inside the basket if it is upside down, or place supports at either side. You may have to suspend it. You can use boxes, other basketforms, or books. Empty weaving cones are excellent because they are narrow, come in many heights, and can be taped or nailed to a board to keep them stable. You have to be very flexible in finding the proper support aid for the particular situation.

STRUCTURAL PRINCIPLES IN BASKETRY

It is necessary to understand a number of structural principles in sculptural basketweaving: balance, stress, weight, and strength.

The foundation strength, basket weight, and basic structural strength needed in simple baskets still apply, but now there are the principles of the center of balance, cross structuring, and the extra stresses imposed by working in asymmetrical form.

Center of Balance. The center of balance is very important when building an asymmetrical piece. As the central axis changes, the weight shifts. Equal weight must be planned for each side. More weight must be placed on the light side of the central axis area to compensate for the extra weight or extensions on the other.

To find the center of balance of the axis, a line can be drawn up through the piece, and the weight must be equal on both sides. If you have extensions on one side and not on the other, make the extended side more open, and the other side more solid and heavy. If the piece will not balance properly, see if you can add extra weight to the light side.

Murphy presented two problems in weight and center of balance (see color photo page 131). First, in order to equalize his center of balance, his body had to be extended over the top of the tail section. Extra weight was added to the light side by bringing the head back over the upper body again. Second, although he could sit in the proper position with his cylindrical body, he was precarious. The many false legs of the caterpillar were incorporated into long ridges that were placed along Murphy's base to provide the needed support for his fat round body.

If you are not sure how to balance the weight, use clay to find a balance point in your form. Duplicate the shape, and see what you can add to the light side of the clay form that can be transferred to the basket. The clay will help you to get the feel of the weight and the balance involved. Bending coat hanger wire into shapes will help you with balance as well in a more open structure. Try some asymmetrical shapes to see what has to be done to equalize the center of balance. You may have to compromise your original idea somewhat to work it out.

When making a basketry piece, you usually hold it in your hands or lap as you work unless it is very large. Place it down from time to time to check the balance and planned direction.

Weight and Foundation Strength. Although foundation strength is necessary for any piece that has size and weight, it is even more important in freeform pieces. The weight in contemporary work can become a problem with some materials, and sufficient foundation strength must be built in. This can be handled in several ways.

Since some core materials are heavier than others (although the diameter may be the same), the core chosen for the foundation or stress areas can be heavier than those chosen for the upper portion of the work. If the allover core material is light, will the base be heavy enough to anchor down a piece of some size? Larger cores can be used with the change of size in mind. The piece must be planned so the core change is expected and pleasing to the eye. If you do not want to make an apparent change in look, but you need more weight, an inner shell of heavier material can be made either before or after the foundation is made. This inner shell can be attached as often or seldom as desired. If you wish to use the same material throughout the basket for the core, be sure the base is structured to carry the weight and balance.

Wrap materials must also be chosen for strength. If the core is heavy, the wrap material must be heavy enough to support the core weight. Since wrap is the "glue" that holds the piece together, choose heavy nonelastic materials. The wrapping must be tight. If the chosen wrap is light, double or triple the strands for more strength.

Use more fastenings in the rows that are strategic. Continuous figure-eight rows should be used at critical points such as: lifting from the base, surrounding the base of the neck, supporting an extension from the piece, or any point where weight is being carried above, and any point where openings occur.

The strongest weave is the basic figure-eight. Since the wrap weaves move, if they are used for decorative patterns they must be supported by accompanying figure-eights where extra strength is needed. The exclusive use of figure-eights in sculptural work eliminates extra difficulties and helps you to concentrate on the structuring problems involved without having to worry about special weaves. Special weaves can be saved for special effects and textures.

Stress and Cross Structuring. Cross structuring is one of the ways to support the basket in points of stress. It is the process of working rows back and forth across an area perpendicular to the surrounding work.

Cross structuring was needed in making both Sidney and Clarence. Sidney's shell was made in two pieces. If the connecting rows had been woven in the same direction, the weight of the shells would have folded and collapsed at the junction area. Cross structuring was used to push the shell sides apart. The outside edges further helped to strengthen the junction areas (see the top photo on page 157).

Sidney (above). 16" x 8" x 7" diameter (40.64cm x 20.32cm x 17.78cm). The natural progression of coiled basketry develops into the snail shell shape. Woven in basic figure-eight over jute core, it is constructed in five separate pieces which are woven together. The shell shows the cross structuring which is used to strengthen the shell construction.

Twined Plaque with Looped Edge. 10" diameter x 1" (25.40cm x 2.54cm). This twined piece is an experiment to show the beauty of the basket center, and how it can be incorporated into a wall hanging. Although this piece is only twining with looped warp ends, it suggests ideas of how it can be used with coiling and plaiting.

Clarence's lower shell was cross structured to push out his legs as well as the sides of the upper shell.

Doubling the thickness of walls at points of stress will provide extra support. This extra support gives a bas-relief look to the basket if the doubling is on the surface.

USING COLOR IN SCULPTURAL WORK

As stated before, color can detract from work if it is not handled properly. Nature gives the male bird bright plumage to make him attractive, but the female is dressed in neutral colors to help her hide and protect herself and her brood from predators.

Bright colors can make a basket a focal point. If the contents are to be more important than the basket, the basket should move into the background by using more neutral colors.

When working sculpturally, the activity of the work itself can become confusing when adding too many colors. It is best to use only one color and sometimes two in busy sculptural pieces. More colors can be incorporated if they are used as a surface design when the activity of the coiling occurs on the same plane.

Surface design used on the slightly convex plane of the Mandala Shield works well. When the colors spill over into the separate units at the side, the separation between the units allows more colors to be accepted (see right side photo on page 131).

If the activity is built up on the surface in a twisted bas-relief effect, more than one color can become confusing.

COMBINING DIFFERENT TECHNIQUES

Twining can be used for the centers of wall hangings with coiling on the outside edge. After the beautiful twined center begins to flatten out about an inch (2.54cm) or two beyond the strap joinings, the coiling can begin (see the bottom photo on page 157).

The warp ends can be finished off on the back of the work, or they can rise out of the surface or be brought back to the surface through slits. These ends can be used in surface weaving on the coiled edge.

It would be difficult to build a twined piece on the outside of a coiled start, but warps could be wrapped and used as surface coiling that would then extend over the edge as twined work. A strip of coiling could be placed between the basket center and the outside edge of a twined piece. There are many ways these two techniques can be used.

Plaiting can be used as a weaving process with the coiled and twined techniques. Flat leather plaiting could be surrounded by coiling, or used as a liner for a coiled basket. Many of the ancient baskets were double-walled using two different techniques. The beautiful fishing boats used on the lakes of southern India are twined on the outside for strength and plaited on the inside for comfort.

Basketweaving can also be used with tapestry weaving in many ways. Placing it on the weaving surface, forming the weaving around it, or weaving in a basketwoven frame are but a few ideas. Braiding, macrame, knotting, and laces can be combined with it as well (see the photo on page 146).

BUILDING RAPPORT WITH YOUR WORK

There are times when you will want to use an idea that, no matter how hard you try, does not work. When this happens, you need to stop and listen to your piece. Put it where you can see it often. Every time you pass, stop and look and listen. The piece will communicate with you.

This advice may sound strange if you have never done it, but you and your work do cooperate to create something beautiful. As a child is created by his parents to become a separate individual, not an extension of his parents, so your work becomes something separate and individual, not just an extension of you. You must become very objective.

Sometimes the piece will tell you to continue in the way you are going, but with a slight variation. Sometimes you must remove parts that do not work.

Moving away from the piece allows your influence to dissipate, and the personality of the piece becomes stronger as it is able to be seen and heard. Listen to it. Learn to feel your work both tactually and emotionally.

When you come back to work, you will be better able to listen, to see, and to feel. You and your piece will become equalized again, and you will be able to work better together. Together you will create something you both like, something with which you both can feel comfortable.

Glossary

Basic Figure-Eight. Coiled weave in which the wrap material is formed into a figure-eight shape around two rows of core to fasten them together.

Basket Base. Base of a coiled basket.

Basket Center. Beginning of a twined basket.

Basket Start. Beginning circle or oval in a coiled basket.

Beading Weave. Overlay of material fastened to the previous rows in coiled basketry.

Blanket Weave. Also known as the buttonhole weave, similar to the blanket or buttonhole stitch in embroidery.

Butterfly. Figure-eight grouping of materials keeping them workable without tangling.

Center Point. Point where the end of the core meets the working core for the first time in a coiled basket.

Center Point Line. Imaginary line drawn from the center point to the outside edge of the base.

Coil. A loop of wrapped core which crosses over itself.

Coiled Basketry. Technique which is made by building one row on top of the last in a continuing spiral.

Core. Cylindrical material which is wrapped in coiled basketry.

Cross Warping. Twining technique in which the center straps are placed like spokes of a wheel before fastening them together.

Cycloids. Coils made perpendicular to the previous row creating a decorative row or edge for the coiled basket.

Erratic Twining. A regular or irregular design which undulates on the surface of a twined basket.

Fastening Down. Process of fastening two rows together in coiled basketry.

Featherstitch Braiding. Type of leather lacing which makes a beautiful edge for a plaited basket.

Filigree Looping. Series of perpendicular loops placed on a coiled basketry row to form a decorative row or edge.

Full Twist. When a pair of strands are twisted a full turn to keep the back color in place in twining.

Half Twist. When a pair of strands are twisted a half turn to bring the back color forward for a design change in twining. The process used in weaving a twined row.

Holding Hand. The nonwriting or nondominant hand.

Imbrication. Overlapping of materials on a coiled or plaited basket.

Interlocking. When weft materials approach each other from opposite directions and loop around each other before reversing direction.

Knot Weave. Variation similar to the traditional knot or mariposa weave, except a knot is formed on the inside as well as the outside of the basket.

Lace Weave. This weave is also known as the Samoan weave.

Lift Point. Point where the coiled basket begins to lift from the base.

Lift Point Line. Imaginary line drawn from the lift point to the top of the basket.

Long Wrap. Wrap which crosses over and fastens the new core to the previous row in the coiled wrap weaves.

Loop. Wrapped core bent or curled without crossing itself.

Open Wrap Weaves. Weaves used over attractive cores to allow the core to show through.

Patterned Wrap Weave. This weave is also known as the Peruvian coil.

Pebble Weave. Knot weave made without holding the rows apart.

Plaiting. Weaving technique in which the warp and weft cross each other in perpendicular fashion.

Pierced Figure Eight. A weave similar to the bee-skep. Figure-eight which picks up the wrap or pierces the top of the previous row core.

Pleated Weave. Variation of the Klikitat weave; pleated material which overlays the previous row in a coiled basket.

Post. Long wrap in the wrap weave variations in coiling which are wrapped to make the knot.

Ripple Weave. Also known as the Shi-lo, a weave made with two cores of different diameters.

Surface Coiling. Decorative bas relief composed of loops and coils fastened to the basket surface.

Taper Cut. Warps and cores cut at an angle.

Traditional Wrap Weave. Wrap fastened around or through the previous row every wrap.

Twining. Weaving with two strands of weft which twist around each other between each warp and then separate to pass the warp on opposite sides.

Warp. The vertical skeleton of the plaited or twined basket.

Weft. The weaving material used in plaited or twined baskets.

Wigwam Weave. Wrap weave variation with several posts.

Working Hand. The dominant or writing hand.

Woven Center. The center straps of the twined basket are woven before they are fastened together.

Wrap. Material which covers the core in coiled baskets.

Wrap Weave. Coiled weave which wraps the new core to the previous row without a change of direction. The random placement of the wraps is also known as the Lazy Squaw, and the patterned placement is also known as the Peruvian coil.

Suppliers List

Cane and Basket Supply
1283 South Cochran Avenue
Los Angeles, California 90019
(catalog) cane, reed, rattan,
sea grass, raffia, etc.

Creative Handweavers
P.O. Box 26480
Los Angeles, California 90026
(catalog) unusual items, imported
yarns, munj, coïr, jute, etc.

International Handcraft & Supply
1550 Westwood Boulevard
Los Angeles, California 90024
(no catalog) jutes, macrame
braids, linens, waxed linens,
coïr, etc.

Tandy Leather Company # 7307
7661 Grapevine Highway
Fort Worth, Texas 76118
(catalog) complete leather
supply stores throughout the
country

All these stores will mail order.

Index